REGENTS RENAISSANCE DRAMA SERIES

General Editor: Cyrus Hoy
Advisory Editor: G. E. Bentley

THE FAWN

JOHN MARSTON

The Fawn

Edited by

GERALD A. SMITH

LONDON
EDWARD ARNOLD (PUBLISHERS) LTD.

Printed in Great Britain by
William Clowes and Sons, Limited, London and Beccles

Regents Renaissance Drama Series

The purpose of the Regents Renaissance Drama Series is to provide soundly edited texts, in modern spelling, of the more significant plays of the Elizabethan, Jacobean, and Caroline theater. Each text in the series is based on a fresh collation of all sixteenth- and seventeenth-century editions. The textual notes, which appear above the line at the bottom of each page, record all substantive departures from the edition used as the copy-text. Variant substantive readings among sixteenth- and seventeenth-century editions are listed there as well. In cases where two or more of the old editions present widely divergent readings, a list of substantive variants in editions through the seventeenth century is given in an appendix. Editions after 1700 are referred to in the textual notes only when an emendation originating in some one of them is received into the text. Variants of accidentals (spelling, punctuation, capitalization) are not recorded in the notes. Contracted forms of characters' names are silently expanded in speech prefixes and stage directions, and, in the case of speech prefixes, are regularized. Additions to the stage directions of the copy-text are enclosed in brackets. Stage directions such as "within" or "aside" are enclosed in parentheses when they occur in the copy-text.

Spelling has been modernized along consciously conservative lines. "Murther" has become "murder," and "burthen," "burden," but within the limits of a modernized text, and with the following exceptions, the linguistic quality of the original has been carefully preserved. The variety of contracted forms (*'em, 'am, 'm, 'um, 'hem*) used in the drama of the period for the pronoun *them* are here regularly given as *'em*, and the alternation between *a'th'* and *o'th'* (for *on* or *of the*) is regularly reproduced as *o'th'*. The copy-text distinction between preterite endings in *-d* and *-ed* is preserved except where the elision of *e* occurs in the penultimate syllable; in such cases, the final syllable is contracted. Thus, where the old editions read "threat'ned," those of the present series read "threaten'd." Where, in the old editions, a contracted preterite in *-y'd* would yield *-i'd* in modern spelling (as in "try'd," "cry'd," "deny'd"), the word is here given in its full form (e.g., "tried," "cried," "denied").

Punctuation has been brought into accord with modern practices. The effort here has been to achieve a balance between the generally light pointing of the old editions, and a system of punctuation which, without overloading the text with exclamation marks, semicolons, and dashes, will make the often loosely flowing verse (and prose) of the original syntactically intelligible to the modern reader. Dashes are regularly used only to indicate interrupted speeches, or shifts of address within a single speech.

Explanatory notes, chiefly concerned with glossing obsolete words and phrases, are printed below the textual notes at the bottom of each page. References to stage directions in the notes follow the admirable system of the Revels editions, whereby stage directions are keyed, decimally, to the line of the text before or after which they occur. Thus, a note on 0.2 has reference to the second line of the stage direction at the beginning of the scene in question. A note on 115.1 has reference to the first line of the stage direction following line 115 of the text of the relevant scene.

CYRUS HOY

University of Rochester

Contents

Abbreviations

Bullen — *The Works of John Marston*. Ed. A. H. Bullen. 3 vols. London, 1887.

corr. — corrected

Deighton — K. Deighton. *Marston's Works: Conjectural Readings*. London, 1893.

Dilke — *Old English Plays*. Ed. Charles W. Dilke. 2 vols. London, 1814–1816.

Florio — John Florio, *A World of Words, or Dictionary of the Italian and English Tongues*. London, 1611.

Juvenal — *Juvenal and Persius*. Trans. G. G. Ramsay. Loeb Classical Library. London and New York, 1918.

Montaigne — *Essayes* Trans. John Florio. Ed. J. I. M. Stewart. Modern Library Edition. New York, 1933.

N&Q — *Notes and Queries*

OED — *Oxford English Dictionary*

Onions — C. T. Onions. *Shakespeare Glossary*. Oxford, 1946.

Ovid — *Heroides and Amores*. Trans. Grant Showerman. Loeb Classical Library. London and New York, 1914. *Metamorphoses*. Trans. Frank J. Miller. 2 vols. Loeb Classical Library. London and Cambridge, Mass., 1936. *Remedia Amoris*, in *Ovid, the Art of Love and Other Poems*. Trans. J. H. Mozley. Loeb Classical Library. London and New York, 1929.

Persius — See Juvenal

Plutarch — *The Lives of the Noble Grecians and Romans*. Trans. John Dryden. Modern Library Edition. New York, n.d.

PMLA — *Publications of the Modern Language Association of America*

Q1 — First Quarto of 1606

Q2 — Second Quarto of 1606 ("corrected of many faults, which by reason of the Author's absence were let slip in the first edition")

Quintilian — *The Institutio Oratoria of Quintilian*. Trans. H. E. Butler. 4 vols. Loeb Classical Library. London and New York, 1921–1922.

S.D.	Stage direction
Seneca	*Thyestes*. Trans. Ella Harris in *The Complete Roman Drama*. Ed. George Duckworth. 2 vols. New York, 1942.
S.P.	Speech prefix
Taylor	Archer Taylor. "Proverbs and Proverbial Phrases in the Plays of John Marston," *Southern Folklore Quarterly*, XXIV (September 1960), 193–216.
Tilley	Morris P. Tilley. *A Dictionary of Proverbs in England in the Sixteenth and Seventeenth Centuries*. Ann Arbor, 1950.
uncorr.	uncorrected
Virgil	*Aeneid*. Ed. W. R. Harper and F. J. Miller. New York and Chicago, 1892.
Wood	*The Plays of John Marston*. 3 vols. London and Edinburgh, 1934–1939.
1633	*Works of J. Marston*. Ed. William Sheares. London, 1633.

Introduction

Marston's *Parasitaster*, or *The Fawn*, was first played sometime between February 4, 1604, and March 12, 1606. The first of these dates is fixed as a result of the advertisement that appeared on the title page when the play was presented by the company known as The Children of the Queen's Majesty's Revels. Since Queen Anne, wife of James I, did not officially patronize this company of boys until February 4, 1604, they would not have used the Queen's name before that date.[1] The other terminus, March 12, 1606, is the date on which the play was entered for publication by William Cotton in the Stationer's Register: "A playe called the Ffaune provided that he shall not put the same in print before he gett alowed lawfull aucthoritie."

Several circumstances point to 1604 rather than 1605 as the year of first production. Marston was probably too busy in 1605 to write this play. In that year, he wrote part of *Eastward Ho*, and perhaps *The Dutch Courtesan*. As a result of the insults offered the King in *Eastward Ho*, Ben Jonson and George Chapman, Marston's collaborators, were thrown into prison and Marston fled London in order to escape imprisonment. The troubles over *Eastward Ho* led Edward Kirkham, one of the managers of the company of the Queen's Revels, to leave the company in order to take a similar post with the Paul's Boys. Since the notice on the title page of the second edition of *The Fawn* states that the play was acted by both companies, Sir Edmund Chambers has pointed out that Kirkham probably took the play with him when he left the company.[2]

The main plot, in which Dulcimel tricks her "all-wise" father into acting as naive go-between in her love affair with Tiberio, may be indebted in its general lines to the third story of the third day in Boccaccio's *Decameron*. But if so, Marston considerably improved upon Boccaccio. Boccaccio's woman was already married and used

---

[1] Anthony Caputi, *John Marston, Satirist* (Ithaca, N.Y., 1961), p. 268.
[2] *Elizabethan Stage* (Oxford, 1951), III, 432; cf. Caputi, pp. 267–268.

an honest friar as the innocent messenger and counselor to whom she complained about the imaginary advances of the man she wished to woo. When the friar reproved the man on several occasions, the man finally recognized the woman's advances and found a way to act upon her suggestions. But Marston's situation is much more amusing. Dulcimel's innocent messenger is her father, Gonzago, who is eagerly promoting her marriage to the elderly Duke of Ferrara for political reasons. At the same time, he is firmly discouraging her attraction to the Duke's son, Tiberio, who is acting as agent for his father.

Marston did not need Boccaccio as a source. The duped father is also present in Chapman's *All Fools*, and Chapman's play is itself based on Terence's *Adelphi*. Later, Molière was to use the situation in *L'Ecole des Maris*. The secondary plot, in which a duke assumes a disguise in order to observe for himself the corruption of a court, is similar to several contemporary plays: Shakespeare's *Measure for Measure*, Marston's own *What You Will* and *The Malcontent*, and Middleton's *The Phoenix*. The epilogue to *The Fawn* tells us that the play is a "slight scene" and that its weakness is the result of a faulty style, plot, and spirit. But such apologies are the conventional modesty of the gentleman-poet and are not to be taken seriously. Although not mighty drama, *The Fawn* is a clever satire.

Satire was officially disapproved by James I, as it had been by Elizabeth I. In Elizabeth's reign, Marston's early satiric poetry had been publicly burned; in James's reign, he was twice sentenced to jail. Since Marston was familiar with the official attitudes toward satire, the Prologue to *The Fawn* is careful to announce that "here no rude disgraces/ Shall taint a public, or a private name" (ll. 5–6). Despite such disavowal of satirical aim, A. W. Upton was able to see Gonzago as a caricature of the king.[3] Sir Edmund Chambers places *The Fawn* with a group of plays between 1604 and 1606 that got the company or the playwrights into trouble with the authorities: *Philotas*, *Eastward Ho*, *The Dutch Courtesan*. Oddly enough, these were the plays produced by the company that was patronized by the Queen.[4]

---

[3] "Allusions to James I and His Court in *The Fawne*," *PMLA*, XLIV (1929), 1048–1065.
[4] Caputi, p. 204.

Therefore, the disclaimer of satiric intent may not be taken too seriously. Although the principal action of *The Fawn* is the love affair between Tiberio and Dulcimel, much of the interest lies in the enveloping activities, the Fawn's exposure of all the fops, flatterers, lovers, and pompous politicians of the court. Many of the minor characters—Nymphadoro, Herod Frappatore, Sir Amoroso Debile-Dosso—play small parts in the play, but serve delightfully as exemplars of the petty, foolish, and fraudulent people who infest courts.

The name of the central character, Fawn or Faunus, suggests a variety of roles. In addition to a fawner, or, as the alternative title of the quarto editions has it, a parasitaster (imitation parasite), a flatterer, a sycophant, the name also suggests a classical giver of oracles and a Renaissance forest figure, the satyr. As such, Faunus follows a line of similar stage figures at the turn of the seventeenth century: Jonson's Macilente, Shakespeare's Jaques and Vincentio, Middleton's Phoenix, and Marston's own Feliche and Quadratus. Like these other characters, the Fawn argues that the best governments are those which permit free speech, and especially honest satire:

> Most spotless kingdom,
> And men, O happy born under good stars,
> Where what is honest you may freely think,
> Speak what you think, and write what you do speak,
> Not bound to servile soothings. (I.ii.319–323).

The Fawn himself does not indulge in political or religious satire. His role and his point of view are not those of a general commentator on the present unhappy state of affairs. Instead, he is one of the actors in the drama, the wise central character who reveals and exhibits the folly of the others by imitating them. In his long soliloquy at the end of the first act, he explains his position and function in the play. He has now been made aware, as a former prince, how dangerous it is for a prince to suppress satire:

> I think a prince
> Whose tender sufferance never felt a gust
> Of bolder breathings, but still liv'd gently fann'd
> With the soft gales of his own flatterers' lips,
> Shall never know his own complexion. (I.ii.306–310).

Since it is flatterers who prevent princes from knowing themselves, the Fawn vows to practice flattery himself in order to expose flattery.

He will revenge himself upon flatterers by flattering them until shame forces them to abandon their vice:

> But since our rank
> Hath ever been afflicted with these flies
> (That blow corruption on the sweetest virtues),
> I will revenge us all upon you all
> With the same stratagem we still are caught,
> Flattery itself . . . (I.ii.323–328).

He plays his disguised part with a vengeance. He eggs on the flatterers to more flattery, the braggarts to bigger brags, the lovers to grander boasts, the pseudo-learned to more impressive appraisals of their wisdom. He also enjoys playing his part: no longer is he Hercules, the upright duke, making his way by strength, honesty, and fair dealing; he is Faunus, the slippery sycophant, who climbs by lying, flattery, and fraud.

By announcing his disguise and the means by which he will expose evil, the Fawn lets the audience enjoy with him the pleasure of his rich revenge. The central character in the satire has now been altered from snarling reformer into clever and witty practitioner of the vices which he wishes to expose. Nymphadoro, one of the characters exposed, soon notices the difference: "He hath gotten more lov'd reputation of virtue, of learning, of all graces, in one hour, than all your snarling reformers have in—" (II.i.14–16). The Fawn's attempt as Parasitaster has been successful, and Herod praises him for dropping the older commentator's posture of snarling reformer: ". . . what a filling of Danae's tub, is it become to inveigh against folly! Community takes away the sense, and example the shame. . . . A stoical sour virtue seldom thrives" (II.i.17–23).

But Marston is not completely content to drop his former stance as sharp satirist. He introduces a seemingly stupid fool, Dondolo, who, in the space of thirty lines in the first scene of Act IV (ll. 176–205), makes a list of easily recognizable types for inclusion in the freight of the ship of fools. Dondolo complains about justices of the peace, great politicians, and priests. He also makes fun of critics who fish at the measure of Plautus' verses (an example from Montaigne of the foolish pursuits of scholars), and poets who try to establish the true spelling and pronunciation of *laughing*. Dondolo also says that the Duke labored hard to ship all fools out of his kingdom because he "would play the fool himself alone, without any rival". Such talk goes too far, might offend the king, and the Fawn warns, "'Ware your breech, fool". Marston has done well to assign the sharp satire to the fool. The fool is protected by custom and privilege: "'tis the privilege of poor fools to talk before an intelligencer" (IV.i.222–223). But the sharp satire is brief; most of the wit is directed at the foolish characters in the play rather than at figures outside the play.

Sir Amoroso Debile-Dosso is perhaps the best example of the humorous butt of a private-theater comedy. He complains about his inability to charm his sour-faced wife, Donna Garbetza, and his inability to father his desired son and heir. The discussions of his aphrodisiac remedies and the jokes directed against his debility show a genial facet of the Fawn and Marston's skill in the sort of sick humor which would appeal to the titter sector of the sophisticated audience at the Blackfriars. Garbetza, as the bitter wife who revenges herself on her husband, Sir Amoroso, by carrying on an adulterous affair with her brother-in-law, Herod, is properly punished by having the Fawn reveal that Herod is also making love to a laundress, Puttota. In the exposure scene, the audience enjoys the indignant Garbetza suffering the death of her social pretensions while Herod is begging the Fawn not to read the letters he has written to Puttota. Since Herod has previously been willing to brag about his affair with Garbetza, the punishment is highly appropriate and therefore highly amusing.

The arrangements between Don Zuccone and his wife, Donna Zoya, are the material for several scenes. Don Zuccone brags about his four-year separation from his wife's favors. Then he is crazy with jealousy and anger when he discovers that the court is full of gossip that she is with child. She soon reveals to the audience that she has started the rumors herself in order to revel in Zuccone's excitement when he hears them. The Fawn adds to this situation by convincing Zuccone that he should divorce Donna Zoya. In a subsequent scene we see Donna Zoya begging on her knees to be forgiven while Zuccone scorns and condemns her. All this is in preparation for the final scene at the Parliament of Cupid in which Donna Zoya's deception is revealed to Zuccone and he must, in his turn, beg her forgiveness. She scorns him in the same fashion in which she has been scorned. She finally forgives him only after he has promised in great detail, and with many specific provisions, never to be suspicious or jealous again.

Nymphadoro is satirized as the universal lover, "a perfect Ovidian". The Fawn listens as, in identical phrases, he assures both Donetta and Garbetza that she is his greatest love. He tells the Fawn that he loves some nineteen ladies, but that Dulcimel is his highest aim, since she combines beauty with fortune. The Fawn gives his opinions of Nymphadoro's loves by his descriptions of the ugliness of Donetta and Garbetza, the two to whom Nymphadoro pledges his love on stage.

Gonzago is a more elaborate example of a satiric gull. On the one side, he is a close imitation of the recent stage favorite, Polonius. Like Polonius, he is a father who is very fond of pointing out that age is synonymous with wisdom. He has also learned a bit of classical lore and rhetoric in school and never tires of exhibiting them. He preens himself and announces that he is philosopher, orator, poet, politician, and statesman: "My Lord Granuffo, pray ye note my phrase" (I.ii.91). As Polonius notes that brevity is the soul of wit, Gonzago tells us, at the end of a long, windy speech, "wise heads use but few words." As a poet, Gonzago is reminiscent of the jokes about Ben Jonson and his difficulties with rhymes: ". . . dash'd the drifts . . . past his shifts ('fore Jove! we could make a good poet)" (V.i.130–132). As a scholar, Gonzago is fond of talking about "we learned" who have read Pliny.

The audience in the theater must have eagerly awaited the Parliament of Cupid in which all of these satirized characters are fully exposed, and made to confess and beg forgiveness for their follies and vices. Each of the braggarts and flatterers is brought forward—Sir Amoroso, Nymphadoro, Zuccone—confronted with the people he has deceived, and ordered aboard the ship of fools. Granuffo is made to confess that he has seemed wise by keeping silent, and the stage is prepared for the exposure of Gonzago. He is first made to admit that anyone who had opposed the match of two young lovers and yet been deceived into bringing them together must be an outstanding fool. When Tiberio and Dulcimel are discovered above, hand in hand, he admits that there is no folly to compare with professed wit. Hercules, dropping his disguise as the Fawn, agrees heartily, and the satire comes to a pleasant close.

Marston himself seems to have been so pleased with the ending that he forgot one of his characters, Philocalia. She was advertised by Nymphadoro as "a lady for Ferrara's Duke: one of great blood, firm age, undoubted honor . . . too excellent to be left unmatch'd, though few worthy to match with her" (III.i.156–159). But Marston fails to fulfill our expectations. At the beginning of the last act she is waiting above with Tiberio and Dulcimel and the priest, but when they descend at the end of the play, Philocalia has disappeared.

Despite this small slip, Marston's play achieves its main intent: it is an amusing satire which makes good fun of some of the sillier courtier types. Its caricatures, including that of the duke, Gonzago, are broad enough to serve their merry purposes. The love-intrigue is predictable, but the anticipation fills the ladies with delight as woman again brings man to his knees. Bright repartee and popular wisdom of the Montaigne variety keep the texture of the dialogue bright and witty. The ridicule of the immoralists by the Parasitaster satisfies the moral instincts of the same audience which enjoys the frank and loose talk of the fops. The fashionable audience must have left the Blackfriars Theatre with a feeling of affection for the author. As he admits at the end of the Epilogue, such affection was all that Marston desired:

> he ever hath aspir'd
> To be belov'd, rather than admir'd.

THE TEXT

The two quartos of *The Fawn* were printed in 1606 by Thomas Purfoot, Jr., who had printed Marston's *The Dutch Courtesan* in 1605. The two quartos of *The Fawn* are not completely separate editions; the type of nine of the eighteen formes of the first quarto was re-impressed in whole or in part in order to print the second quarto. That is, thirty-eight of its seventy pages were reset for Q2, but thirty-two pages were corrected and re-impressed. Since the corrections were made between the editions, even when some of them could have been made within Q1, it seems likely that Purfoot tried to deceive the reading public into believing that there were two quartos, when, in fact, nearly half of Q2 was a re-impression of Q1.

Setting and resetting the two quartos in such a short time required the work of two compositors. One of them, whom we shall call Compositor A, set sheets A–D. The second, Compositor B, set sheets E–I. Compositor B's work is easily distinguished from that of Compositor A because he never uses a colon after a speech prefix (A usually does), and he always spells the hero's name with a *w* (Fawne or Fawnus) while A usually (in Q1) spells the hero's name with a *u* (Faunus or Faune). As Martin Wine has pointed out, a similar non-use of the colon after speech prefixes is characteristic of the compositor of the final six formes of *The Dutch Courtesan*.[5] Since the same compositors at the same printing house are probably at work, it appears that Compositor B assumed responsibility for the latter part of each play. Since there were three compositors working on *The Dutch Courtesan*, Compositor B set the last third of that play. Since there were only two compositors doing *The Fawn*, Compositor B set the last half. The spelling of the running titles points to the same division of labor: Compositor B spells courtesan "Curtezan," a spelling never used by the other compositors. In *The Fawn*, Compositor B often uses a swash *A*, a practice which the other compositor did not follow.

Although we can identify the work of the compositors, the identification does not help us very much with the establishment of the text. Practically nothing is known about the compositorial habits of these compositors; therefore an editor has little evidence on which to decide whether or not a given compositor has made a specific error. But the identification of the compositors does help with the problem of the standing type, and perhaps it helps with the problem of the size of the editions. When the second quarto was begun, Compositor A was near the end of his part of the typesetting. He left the final sheet (D) and a page (sig. C1) of his part standing in readiness for Q2. Likewise, Compositor B was near the end of his part; he left his final sheet (I), the inner formes of the two next-to-last sheets (G and H) and sig. G1 standing. The standing-type pages were corrected and re-impressed for Q2. The other pages were reset line-by-line from a corrected copy of Q1 for Q2. The only exception to the pattern of leaving the final pages of each compositor's part standing was the title page and introductory material of sheet A (sigs. A1, A2, A2ᵛ, A3ᵛ).[6] This exception is at least partly customary: it was often the practice to leave the title page standing so that it could be used separately as an advertisement for the book.

Q1 is the only edition which derives directly from the author's manuscript. Therefore, this edition uses Q1 as copy-text. But Q2 also has textual authority because it was corrected by the author. When there is a substantive variance between Q1 and Q2, the reading of Q2 is usually adopted. But each variant is a separate

---

[5] "The Dutch Courtesan: A Critical Edition" (unpub. Harvard diss., 1960), p. 575.

[6] See Robert E. Brettle, "Marston Bibliography—a Correction," *The Library*, XV (1934–1935), pp. 241–242.

editorial problem. A substantive variant may be an authorial correction, but it may also be a compositorial error. Authorial corrections in the re-impressed pages are usually easy to identify, because the compositor will try to make the change by adjusting the type of no more than a line or two. In such cases, the author has probably made the correction and the Q2 reading is the correct one. But in the reset pages, the problem of distinguishing authorial corrections from compositorial errors is much more difficult. Usually the pages are reset line-by-line, but not always. Thus, when an adjustment is made in the length of the line, the variant must be examined closely and as an individual problem.

Not only are some of the variants difficult to establish, there are a great many variants. The textual notes list some 230 variants of all kinds. Approximately 120 of these are substantive variants in which Q2 gives the correct reading. There are about 32 variants which seem to be compositorial errors; in these cases the Q1 reading is preferred. In about 13 cases, the variants are between various copies of Q2. In these cases, there is often some way to show that a given forme of Q2 is a corrected forme. In such cases, the reading of the corrected forme is preferred. A single variant of this variety ("few dons" or "some Lords" at IV.i.320) remains unsolved. This edition's reading, "few dons," is based on the probability that the two extant copies of Q2 which have an uncorrected state of the inner forme of sheet G also have an uncorrected state of the outer forme of the same sheet. But though it seems highly probable that the two formes of the same sheet would be in the same state of correction, Dr. Charlton Hinman has shown that in the Shakespeare First Folio the inner and outer formes of the same sheet are often in different states of correction.[7] Therefore the choice between "few dons" and "some Lords" remains conjectural.

In the variants discussed so far, the choice is within or between Q1 and Q2. Both of the quartos have authority, since one of them is set from the author's manuscript and the other is corrected by the author. But there are some 17 instances in which neither of the quartos seems to have the correct reading. In a few cases, this edition has adopted a reading from *The Works of John Marston*, edited by William Sheares in 1633. Since Marston had nothing to do with the

---

[7] *The Printing and Proof-reading of the First Folio of Shakespeare* (Oxford, 1963), I, 39.

1633 edition, it is not authoritative. Usually the reading of 1633 is identical with the reading of Q1. When there is a choice within Q1, 1633 usually follows the uncorrected Q1. Therefore, in order to avoid cluttering the textual notes, when the reading of 1633 agrees with Q1, it is often omitted. On the other hand, whenever the reading of 1633 shows the difficulty of the choice between variant quarto readings, or sheds even the feeblest light upon that choice, its reading is listed in the textual notes. In still fewer cases, this edition has adopted an emendation of the text by a subsequent editor or made its own emendation. In such cases, the source of the emendation is listed in the textual notes.

The complicated bibliographical and textual situation raises some difficult questions. How, for example, were the booksellers able to sell the first quarto if the second quarto was already available? Why did the printer go to the trouble of preserving the illusion of two editions? The two questions may be related and may be answered by Professor Bowers' opinion that the second quarto was of "dubious legality."[8] If the printer is pretending that there are two editions when there is actually only one and a half, he might be concealing an evasion of the rule of the Stationers' Company that not more than 1500 copies of a book may be printed from a single setting of the type. Bowers strongly suspects an evasion of the law because there were four such books during 1605–1606. Each of the four books had a partly reset second edition which masqueraded as a new edition. Two of the four books were by Dekker (*The Honest Whore*, Part I, and *The Magnificent Entertainment*); the other two were Marston's *The Malcontent* and *The Fawn*.[9]

GERALD A. SMITH

State University of New York
College at Geneseo

---

[8] "Notes on Standing Type in Elizabethan Printing," *Papers of the Bibliographical Society of America*, XL (1946), 222.
[9] *Ibid.*, p. 218.

THE FAWN

TO MY EQUAL READER

I have ever more endeavored to know myself than to be known of others; and rather to be unpartially beloved of all, than factiously to be admired of a few. Yet so powerfully have I been enticed with the delights of poetry, and (I must ingeniously confess) above better desert so fortunate 5 in these stage-pleasings, that (let my resolutions be never so fixed to call mine eyes into myself) I much fear that most lamentable death of him,

> Qui nimis notus omnibus,
> Ignotus moritur sibi. —Seneca. 10

But since the over-vehement pursuit of these delights hath been the sickness of my youth, and now is grown to be the vice of my firmer age, since to satisfy others, I neglect myself, let it be the courtesy of my peruser, rather to pity my self-hind'ring labors than to malice me, and let him be 15 pleased to be my reader, and not my interpreter, since I would fain reserve that office in my own hands, it being my daily prayer: Absit à jocorum nostrorum simplicitate malignus interpres. —Martial.

If any shall wonder why I print a comedy, whose life rests 20 much in the actor's voice, let such know that it cannot avoid publishing. Let it therefore stand with good excuse, that I have been my own setter out.

If any desire to understand the scope of my comedy, know it hath the same limits which Juvenal gives to his satires: 25

> Quicquid agunt homines, votum, timor, ira, voluptas,
> Gaudia, discursus, nostri farrago libelli est. —Juvenal.

As for the factious malice and studied detractions of some few that tread in the same path with me, let all know I most easily neglect them, and (carelessly slumb'ring to 30

---

5. *ingeniously*] ingenuously.
9–10. *Qui . . . sibi*] "Who dies but too well known to all the world, yet knowing not himself" (Seneca, *Thyestes*, 395–396).
18–19. *Absit . . . interpres*] "May the frankness of my jests find no malicious interpreter" (Martial, Preface to the *Epigrams*).
26–27. *Quicquid . . . est*] "All the doings of mankind—their vows, their

their vicious endeavors) smile heartily at their self-hurting
baseness. My bosom friend, good Epictetus, makes me easily
to contemn all such men's malice. Since other men's tongues
are not within my teeth, why should I hope to govern them?
For mine own interest for once, let this be printed, that of   35
men of my own addiction, I love most, pity some, hate none.
For let me truly say it, I once only loved myself, for loving
them, and surely, I shall ever rest so constant to my first
affection that let their ungentle combinings, discourteous
whisperings, never so treacherously labor to undermine my   40
unfenced reputation, I shall (as long as I have being) love
the least of their graces, and only pity the greatest of their
vices.

And now to kill envy, know you that affect to be the only
minion of Phoebus, I am not so blushlessly ambitious as to   45
hope to gain any the least supreme eminency among you.
I affect not only the "'Euge' tuum et 'Belle'"! 'Tis not my
fashion to think no writer virtuously confident that is not
swellingly impudent. Nor do I labor to be held the only
spirit whose poems may be thought worthy to be kept in   50
cedar chests.

> *Heliconidasque, pallidamque Pyrenen*
> *Illis relinquo quorum imagines lambunt*
> *Hederae sequaces.* . . . —Persius.

He that pursues fame shall for me without any rival have   55
breath enough. I esteem felicity to be a more solid content-
ment; only let it be lawful for me, with unaffected modesty
and full thought, to end boldly with that of Perseus:

45. minion] *Q2;* Minious *Q1.*

---

fears, their angers, and their pleasures, their joys and goings to and fro,
shall form the motley subject of my page" (Juvenal, *Satire* I, 85–86).

41. *unfenced*] defenceless.

47. "'Euge' . . . 'Belle' "] "I decline to admit that the final and supreme
test of excellence is to be found in your 'Bravo!' and your 'Beautiful!'"
(Persius, *Satire* I, 47–49.)

52–54. *Heliconidasque . . . sequaces*] "The maidens of Mount Helicon,
and the blanching waters of Pirene, I give up to the gentlemen round
whose busts the clinging ivy twines" (Persius, Prologue to *Satires,* 4–6.
"relinquo" reads "remitto" in the Ramsay edition).

TO MY EQUAL READER

——Ipse semipaganus
Ad sacra vatum carmen affero nostrum. —Persius.   60
JOHN MARSTON

Reader, know I have perused this copy to make some satisfaction for the first faulty impression; yet so urgent hath been my business, that some errors have still passed, which thy discretion may amend. Comedies are writ to be spoken, 65 not read. Remember the life of these things consists in action, and for your such courteous survey of my pen, I will present a tragedy to you which shall boldly abide the most curious perusal.

62–69. Reader . . . perusal]   *Q2;*
not in Q1.

59–60. *Ipse . . . nostrum*] "It is but as a half-member of the Community that I bring my lay to the holy feast of the bards" (Persius, Prologue to the *Satires*, 6–7).

67–68. *I will . . . tragedy*] Q2 has marginal note, "Sophonisba."

PROLOGUS

Let those once know that here with malice lurk,
'Tis base to be too wise in other's work.
The rest sit thus saluted:
Spectators know, you may with freest faces
Behold this scene, for here no rude disgraces   5
Shall taint a public, or a private name.
This pen at viler rate doth value fame,
Than at the price of others' infamy
To purchase it. Let others dare the rope,
Your modest pleasure is our author's scope.   10
The hurdle and the rack to them he leaves,
That have naught left to be accompted any,
But by not being. Nor doth he hope to win
Your louder hand with that most common sin
Of vulgar pens, rank bawdry, that smells   15
Even through your masks, *usque ad nauseam.*
The Venus of this scene doth loath to wear
So vile, so common, so immodest clothings,
But if the nimble form of comedy,
Mere spectacle of life and public manners,   20
May gracefully arrive to your pleased ears,
We boldly dare the utmost death of fears;
For we do know that this most fair-fill'd room
Is loaden with most Attic judgments, ablest spirits,
Than whom there are none more exact, full, strong,   25
Yet none more soft, benign in censuring.
I know there's not one ass in all this presence,
Not one calumnious rascal, or base villain
Of emptiest merit, that would tax and slander
If innocency herself should write, not one we know't.   30
O you are all the very breath of Phoebus.
In your pleas'd gracings all the true life blood
Of our poor author lives; you are his very graces.
    Now if that any wonder why he's drawn
    To such base soothings, know his play's—*The Fawn.*   35

---

14. louder] *Q2; Laud or Q1.*   34. that] *Q2; not in Q1.*
33. graces] *Q2;* grace *Q1.*

---

16. *usque ad nauseam*] all the way to nausea.   24. *Attic*] learned.

-6-

INTERLOCUTORES

HERCULES, *disguised Faunus, Duke of Ferrara*
GONZAGO, *Duke of Urbin, a weak lord of a self-admiring wisdom*
TIBERIO, *son to Hercules*
DULCIMEL, *daughter to Gonzago*
PHILOCALIA, *an honorable learned lady, companion to the Princess* 5
Dulcimel
GRANUFFO, *a silent lord*
DON ZUCCONE, *a causelessly jealous lord*
DONNA ZOYA, *a virtuous, fair witty lady, his wife*
SIR AMOROSO DEBILE-DOSSO, *a sickly knight* 10
DONNA GARBETZA, *his lady*
HEROD FRAPPATORE, *brother to Sir Amoroso and a vicious braggart*
NYMPHADORO, *a young courtier and a common lover*
DONDOLO, *a bald fool*
RENALDO, *brother to Hercules* 15
POVEIA   ⎫
DONETTA ⎬ *two ladies, attendants on Dulcimel*
PUTTOTA, *a poor laundress of the court that washeth and diets footmen*
PAGES
[CUPID] 20

2. a . . . wisdom] *Q2; not in Q1.*

0.1. *Interlocutores*] speakers.
5. *Philocalia*] "delight in, or love of fairenesse" (Florio, p. 376).
8. *Zuccone*] "a shaven pate, . . . a gull, a ninnic" (Florio, ed. 1598; p. 462).
9. *Zoya* (Zoia) "often used for Gioia" (Florio, p. 616). Florio defines "Gioia" as "a joy, a gemme, a jewell, or any precious thing. Also jouissance, delight, hearts-east, or comfort" (p. 211).
10. *Debile*] "weake, feeble, faint" (Florio, p. 139).
10. *Dosso*] "the backe of a man or any other creature" (Florio, p. 161).
11. *Garbetza*] "sourenesse, tartnesse, sharpnesse" (Florio, p. 204).
12. *Frappatore*] "a bragger, a boaster, a vanter, a cracker. Also a craftie pratler, a cunnicatcher, a cheater" (Florio, p. 196).
13. *Nymphadoro*] (Nimfadoro) "an effeminate fellow, a spruce ladies courting fellow" (Florio, p. 332).
14. *Dondolo*] "a shallow-pate, a silly gull" (Florio, p. 160).
16. *Poveia*] "a Butter-flie or a Ladie-bird" (Florio, p. 394).
17. *Donetta*] "a little woman" (Florio, p. 161).
18. *Puttota*] "a handsome plum cheeked wench" (Florio, p. 412).

The Fawn

Enter Hercules *and* Renaldo. *Dat veniam corvis*
vexat censura
columbas

HERCULES.

See, yonder's Urbin. Those far-appearing spires rise from
the city. You shall conduct me no further. Return to
Ferrara; my dukedom by your care in my absence shall
rest constantly united, and most religiously loyal.

RENALDO.

My prince and brother, let my blood and love challenge   5
the freedom of one question.

HERCULES.

You have't.

RENALDO.

Why, in your steadier age, in strength of life
And firmest wit of time, will you break forth
Those stricter limits of regardful state   10
(Which with severe distinction you still kept)
And now to unknown dangers you'll give up
Yourself, Ferrara's Duke, and in yourself
The state and us? O, my lov'd brother,
"Honor avoids not only just defame,   15
But flies all means that may ill voice his name."

HERCULES.

Busy yourself with no fears, for I shall rest most wary of our
safety; only some glimpses I will give you for your satisfaction why I leave Ferrara. I have vowed to visit the
court of Urbin in some disguise, as thus: my son, as you can   20

0.1–3. *Dat ... columbas*] "Our censor absolves the ravens and passes
judgment on the doves" (Juvenal, *Satire II*, 62–62).

15–16. Sententious utterances are often set off in quotation marks in the
old editions.

–8–

well witness with me, could I never persuade to marriage,
although myself was then an ever-resolved widower, and
though I proposed to him this very lady to whom he is gone
in my right to negotiate. Now how his cooler blood will
behave itself in this business would I have an only testimony. 25
Other contents shall I give myself, as not to take love by at-
torney, or make my election out of tongues. Other sufficings
there are which my regard would fain make sound to me:
something of much you know; that and what else you must
not know, bids you excuse this kind of my departure.   30

RENALDO.

I commend all to your wisdom, and yours to the Wisest.

HERCULES.

Think not but I shall approve that more than folly which
even now appears in a most ridiculous expectation. Be in
this assured: "The bottom of gravity is nothing like
the top." Once more, fare you well.   *Exit* Renaldo. 35
And now, thou ceremonious sovereignty,
Ye proud, severer, stateful complements,
The secret arts of rule, I put you off;
Nor ever shall those manacles of form
Once more lock up the appetite of blood.   40
'Tis now an age of man, whilst we all strict
Have liv'd in awe of carriage regular
Apted unto my place, nor hath my life
Once tasted of exorbitant affects,
Wild longings, or the least of disrank'd shapes.   45
But we must once be wild, 'tis ancient truth.
O fortunate, whose madness falls in youth!
Well, this is text, whoever keeps his place
In servile station, is all low and base.

24. his] *Q1; not in Q2.*   *uncorr.;* onely *1633.*
25. only] *Q1 corr., Q2;* on-a *Q1*

27. *election . . . tongues*] choice by hearsay.
34–35. *The bottom . . . top*] proverbial (Taylor, p. 204).
42. *carriage regular*] proper behavior.
43. *Apted*] natural, appropriate.
44. *affects*] passions.
45. *disrank'd*] disordered.
48. *text*] "a received maxim or axiom" (*OED*).

Shall I because some few may cry, "Light, vain,"   50
Beat down affection from desired rule
(He that doth strive to please the world's a fool),
To have that fellow cry, "O mark him, grave,
See how austerely he doth give example
Of repressed heat and steady life,"   55
Whilst my forc'd life against the stream of blood
Is tugg'd along, and all to keep the God
Of fools and women: nice opinion,
Whose strict preserving makes oft great men fools
And fools oft great men. No, thou world, know thus,   60
"There's nothing free but it is generous."   *Exit.*

[I.ii]   *Enter* Nymphadoro, Herod [*and* Page].

HEROD.

How now, my little more than nothing, what news is
stirring?

PAGE.

All the city's afire—

NYMPHADORO.

On fire?

PAGE.

With joy of the Princess Dulcimel's birthday. There's show   5
upon show, sport upon sport.

HEROD.

What sport, what sport?

PAGE.

Marry, sir, to solemnize the princess' birthday. There's first
crackers which run into the air, and when they are at
the top, like some ambitious strange heretic, keep a-cracking   10
and a-cracking, and then break, and down they come.

HEROD.

A pretty crab! He would yield tart juice and he were
squeez'd.

---

57. tugg'd] *Q2;* lugg'd *Q1.*   60. oft] *Q2;* of *Q1.*

---

56. *stream of blood*] natural inclination.   58. *nice*] precise, delicate.
[I.ii]
    9. *crackers*] fireworks.
    10. *a-cracking*] pun on sense, "bragging."   12. *crab*] crabapple.

NYMPHADORO.

What sport else?

PAGE.

Other fireworks.   15

HEROD.

Spirit of wine, I cannot tell how these fireworks should
be good at the solemnizing the birth of men or women. I
am sure they are dangerous at their begetting. What more
fireworks, sir?

PAGE.

There be squibs, sir; which squibs running upon lines   20
like some of our gaudy gallants, sir, keep a smother, sir,
with flishing and flashing, and in the end, sir, they do, sir—

NYMPHADORO.

What, sir?

PAGE.

Stink, sir.

HEROD.

'Fore heaven, a most sweet youth.   25

Enter Dondolo.

DONDOLO.

News, news, news, news!

HEROD.

What, in the name of prophecy?

NYMPHADORO.

Art thou grown wise?

HEROD.

Doth the duke want no money?

NYMPHADORO.

Is there a maid found at twenty-four?   30

HEROD.

Speak, thou three-legg'd tripos, is thy ship of fools afloat yet?

---

22. *flishing*] flicking.
29. *want*] lack.
31. *three-legg'd tripos*] oracle (the prophetess at Delphi sat on a high
gilded tripod).
31. *ship of fools*] an allusion to Alexander Barclay's translation (1509)
of Sebastian Brandt's *Narrenschiff* (1494).

DONDOLO.

I ha' many things in my head to tell you.

HEROD.

Ay, thy head is always working. It rolls and it rolls, Dondolo, but it gathers no moss, Dondolo.

DONDOLO.

Tiberio, the Duke of Ferrara's son, excellently horsed, 35 all upon Flanders mares, is arrived at the court this very day, somewhat late in the nighttime.

HEROD.

An excellent nuntius.

DONDOLO.

Why, my gallants, I have had a good wit.

HEROD.

Yes, troth, but now 'tis grown like an almanac for the last 40 year, past date; the mark's out of thy mouth, Dondolo.

NYMPHADORO.

And what's the prince's ambassage? Thou art private with the duke; thou belongest to his close stool.

DONDOLO.

Why, every fool knows that. I know it myself, man, as well as the best man. He is come to solicit a marriage betwixt 45 his father, the Duke of Ferrara, and our Duke of Urbin's daughter, Dulcimel.

NYMPHADORO.

Pity of my passions, Nymphadoro shall lose one of his mistresses.

HEROD.

Nay, if thou hast more than one, the loss can ne'er be 50 grievous since 'tis certain he that loves many formally,

---

38. *nuntius*] messenger.

41. *the mark's out of thy mouth*] a horse is often too old for use when the mark, "a depression caused by a fold in the enamel of a horse's incisor tooth" (*OED*), is gone from his mouth.

42. *ambassage*] embassage.

42. *art private with*] have private access to.

43. *close stool*] cf. Montaigne, I, iii, 13: ". . . other Princes, who to dispatch their weightiest affaires make often their close stoole, their regall Throne or Councel-chamber. . . ."

never loves any violently.

NYMPHADORO.

Most trusted Frappatore, is my hand the weaker because it is
divided into many fingers? No, 'tis the more strongly nimble.
I do now love threescore and nine ladies all of them most   55
extremely well, but I do love the princess most extremely
best: but in very sighing sadness, I ha' lost all hope, and with
that hope a lady that is most rare, most fair, most wise, most
sweet, most—

HEROD.

Anything. True, but remember still this fair, this wise,   60
this sweet, this all of excellency has in the tail of all, a
woman.

NYMPHADORO.

Peace, the presence fills against the prince approacheth.
Mark who enters.

HEROD.

My brother, Sir Amoroso Debile-Dosso.   65

NYMPHADORO.

Not he.

HEROD.

No, not he?

NYMPHADORO.

How is he chang'd?

HEROD.

Why, grown the very dregs of the drabs' cup.

NYMPHADORO.

O Babylon, thy walls are fallen. Is he married?   70

HEROD.

Yes, yet still the ladies' common—or the common ladies'—
servant.

NYMPHADORO.

How does his own lady bear with him?

---

63. *presence*] royal "audience" chamber.
63. *against*] in anticipation of.
69. *drab*] prostitute.

HEROD.

    Faith, like the Roman Milo, bore with him when he was a
calf, and now carries him when he's grown an ox.   75

NYMPHADORO.

    Peace, the duke's at hand.

    Cornets. Enter Granuffo, Gonzago, Dulcimel, Philocalia, Poveia.

GONZAGO.

    Daughter, for that our last speech leaves the firmest print,
be thus advis'd. When young Tiberio negotiates his
father's love, hold heedy guard over thy passions, and
still keep this full thought firm in thy reason: 'tis his old 80
father's love the young man moves—[*to Granuffo*] is't
not well thought, my lord? We must bear brain— and when
thou shalt behold Tiberio's life-full eyes and well-fill'd veins,
complexion firm, and hairs that curls with strength of
lusty moisture—[*to Granuffo*] I think we yet can speak, 85
we ha' been eloquent—thou must shape thy thoughts to
apprehend his father well in years,
A grave wise prince, whose beauty is his honor,
And well-pass'd life, and do not give thy thoughts
Least liberty to shape a divers scope—[*to Granuffo*]   90
My Lord Granuffo, pray ye note my phrase—
So shalt thou not abuse thy younger hope,
Nor afflict us, who only joy in life,
To see thee his.

DULCIMEL.

    Gracious my father, fear not; I rest most duteous to your 95
dispose.

              Consort of music.

GONZAGO.

    Set on then, for the music gives us notice the prince is hard
at hand.

    [*Enter*] Tiberio *with his train with* Hercules *disguised* [*as* Faunus].

DULCIMEL.

    You are most welcome to our long-desiring father. To us

76.1. Poveia] *this edn.;* Loia *Q1–2;*
Zoya *Bullen, Wood.*

---

74. *Milo*] Olympic wrestling champion, reputedly able to carry an ox
77. *for that*] because.   77. *print*] imprint.   90. *divers*] diverse.

you are come—   100

TIBERIO.

From our long-desiring father.   *Shows a picture.*

DULCIMEL.

Is this your father's true proportion?

TIBERIO.

No, lady, but the perfect counterfeit.

DULCIMEL.

And the best grac'd—

TIBERIO.

The painter's art could yield.   105

DULCIMEL.

I wonder he would send a counterfeit to move our love.

GONZAGO [*to Granuffo*].

Hear, that's my wit. When I was eighteen old such a pretty
toying wit had I, but age hath made us wise. Hast not,
my lord?

TIBERIO.

Why, fairest princess, if your eye dislike that deader piece, 110
behold me, his true form and livelier image. Such my
father hath been.

DULCIMEL.

My lord, please you to scent this flower.

TIBERIO.

'Tis withered, lady; the flower's scent is gone.

DULCIMEL.

This hath been such as you are, hath been, sir. They say 115
in England that a far-fam'd friar had girt the island round
with a brass wall, if that they could have catched "Time is";
but "Time is past" left it still clipp'd with aged Neptune's
arm.

TIBERIO.

Aurora yet keeps chaste old Tithon's bed.   120

116. fam'd friar] *Q2;* found Frier   118. still] *Q1, Q2 corr.;* hill *Q2*
Q1 corr., 1633; found *Q1 uncorr.*   *uncorr.*

---

118. "*Time . . . past*"] See Robert Greene, *Friar Bacon and Friar Bungay,*
xi.53–75.

118. *clipp'd*] embraced.

DULCIMEL.

Yet blushes at it when she rises.

GONZAGO.

Pretty, pretty. Just like my younger wit. You know it, my
lord.

DULCIMEL.

But is your father's age thus fresh; hath yet his head so
many hairs?   125

TIBERIO.

More, more, by many a one.

DULCIMEL.

More, say you?

TIBERIO.

More.

DULCIMEL.

Right, sir, for this hath none. Is his eye so quick as this
same piece makes him show?   130

TIBERIO.

The courtesy of art hath given more life to that part than
the sad cares of state would grant my father.

DULCIMEL.

This model speaks above forty.

TIBERIO.

Then doth it somewhat flatter, for our father hath seen
more years, and is a little shrunk from the full strength of 135
time.

GONZAGO.

Somewhat coldly prais'd.

DULCIMEL.

Your father hath a fair solicitor;
And be it spoke with virgin modesty,
I would he were no elder. Not that I do fly   140
His side for years, or other hopes of youth,
But in regard the malice of lewd tongues,
Quick to deprave on possibilities,
(Almost impossibilities) will spread
Rumors, to honor dangerous.   145

133. above] *Q2;* about *Q1.*

Dulcimel *and* Tiberio *confer privately.*

GONZAGO.

What? Whisper? Ay, my Lord Granuffo, 'twere fit
To part their lips. Men of discerning wit
That have read Pliny can discourse, or so,
But give me practice; well experienc'd age
Is the true Delphos. I am no oracle,   150
But yet I'll prophesy. Well, my Lord Granuffo,
'Tis fit to interrupt their privacy,
Is't not, my lord? Now sure thou art a man
Of a most learned silence, and one whose words
Have been most precious to me. Right, I know thy heart,   155
'Tis true, thy legs discourse with right and grace,
And thy tongue is constant. —[*To Tiberio.*]   Fair my lord,
Forbear all private closer conference.
What from your father comes, comes openly,
And so must speak: for you must know my age   160
Hath seen the beings and the *quid* of things.
I know *dimensions* and the *termini*
Of all *existens.* Sir, I know what shapes
Appetite forms, but policy and states
Have more elected ends. Your father's suit   165
Is with all public grace received, and private love
Embraced. As for our daughter's bent of mind,
She must seem somewhat nice; 'tis virgin's kind
To hold long out. If yet she chance deny,
Ascribe it to her decent modesty.   170
We have been a philosopher and spoke
With much applause; but now age makes us wise,
And draws our eyes to search the heart of things,
And leave vain seemings. Therefore you must know,
I would be loath the gaudy shape of youth   175
Should one provoke, and not-allow'd-of-heat
Or hinder, or——for, sir, I know, and so.

145.1.] *Q2; not in Q1.*   Q2.
158. all private] *Q1;* all all priuat

161–163. *quid . . . dimensions . . . termini . . . existens*]   essence . . . form . . .
ends . . . being.
165. *elected*] chosen.   168. *nice*] reluctant.

-17-

Therefore before us time and place affords
Free speech, else not. Wise heads use but few words.
In short breath, know the Court of Urbin holds   180
Your presence and your embassage so dear
That we want means once to express our heart
But with our heart. Plain meaning shunneth art.
You are most welcome—Lord Granuffo, a trick,
A figure, note—we use no rhetoric.   [*Exeunt.*] 185

Remanent Hercules, Nymphadoro *and* Herod.

HEROD.
Did not Tiberio call his father fool?
NYMPHADORO.
No, he said years had weaken'd his youthful quickness.
HEROD.
He swore he was bald.
NYMPHADORO.
No, but not thick-hair'd.
HEROD.
By this light, I'll swear he said his father had the hipgout, 190
the strangury, the fistula in *ano*, and a most unabideable
breath; no teeth, less eyes, great fingers, little legs, an
eternal flux, and an everlasting cough of the lungs.
NYMPHADORO.
Fie, fie, by this light he did not.
HEROD.
By this light he should ha' done then. Horn on him, 195
threescore and five, to have and to hold a lady of fifteen.
O Mezentius! a tyranny equal if not above thy torturing.
Thou didst bind the living and the dead bodies together, and
forced them so to pine and rot, but this cruelty binds breast

---

182. express] *Q1;* oppresse *Q2.*   *Gon: Q1-2.*
185. S.D. *Exeunt*] *this edn.; Exit*

185.1. *Remanent*] remain.
191. *strangury*] "a disease of the urinary organs characterized by slow
and painful emission of urine" (*OED*).
193. *flux*] dysentery.
195. *Horn on him*] horns were the symbol of the cuckold.
197. *Mezentius*] expelled as a tyrant by the Tyrrhenians, he was finally
killed by Aeneas (*Aeneid*, Book X).

to breast, not only different bodies, but if it were possible 200
most unequal minds together, with an enforcement even
scandalous to nature.   [*Seeing* Hercules.]   Now the jail
deliver me, an intelligencer! Be good to me ye cloisters
of bondage. Of whence art thou?

HERCULES.

Of Ferrara.   205

HEROD.

A Ferrara's what to me? Camest thou in with the Prince
Tiberio?

HERCULES.

With the Prince Tiberio. What to that? You will not rail
at me, will you?

HEROD.

Who, I? I rail at one of Ferrara, a Ferrarese? No! Didst 210
thou ride?

HERCULES.

No.

HEROD.

Hast thou worn socks?

HERCULES.

No.

HEROD.

Then blessed be the most happy gravel betwixt thy toes. 215
I do prophesy thy tyrannizing itch shall be honorable,
and thy right worshipful louse shall appear in full presence. Art thou an officer to the prince?

HERCULES.

I am, what o' that?

HEROD.

My cap, what officer?   220

HERCULES.

Yeoman of his bottles. What to that?

HEROD.

My lip, thy name good yeoman of the bottles?

217. louse] *Q2 corr.;* Loue *Q2*   218. prince] *Q2;* Princes *Q1.*
uncorr.; soule *Q1.*

---

203. *intelligencer*] spy.

HERCULES.

Faunus.

NYMPHADORO.

Faunus? An old courtier? I wonder thou art in no better
clothes and place, Faunus!   225

HERCULES.

I may be in better place, sir, and with you of more regard
if this match of our duke's intermarriage with the heir of
Urbin proceed, the Duke of Urbin dying, and our lord
coming in his lady's right of title to your dukedom.

HEROD.

Why, then shalt thou, O yeoman of the bottles, become a 230
maker of magnificoes. Thou shalt beg some odd suit, and
change thy old shirt, pare thy beard, cleanse thy teeth,
and eat apricocks, marry a rich widow, or a crack'd lady,
whose case thou shalt make good. Then, my Pythagoras,
shall thou and I make a transmigration of souls. Thou shalt 235
marry my daughter, or my wife shall be thy gracious
mistress. Seventeen punks shall be thy proportion. Thou
shalt beg to thy comfort of clean linen, eat no more fresh
beef at supper, or save the broth for next day's porridge,
but the flesh pots of Egypt shall fatten thee, and the grass- 240
hopper shall flourish in thy summer.

NYMPHADORO.

And what dost thou think of the duke's overture of
marriage?

HEROD.

What do you think?

HERCULES.

May I speak boldly as at Aleppo?   245

NYMPHADORO.

Speak till thy lungs ache, talk out thy teeth; here are
none of those cankers, these mischiefs of society, intelli-

226. you] *Q2;* them *Q1.*   239. save the] *Q2;* haue thy *Q1.*
232. shirt] *Q2;* sute *Q1.*

---

231. *magnificoes*] grandees.
237. *punks*] harlots.
240. *flesh pots of Egypt*] See *Exodus* 16:3.
245. *Aleppo*] a city in northwest Syria.

gencers, or informers, that will cast rumor into the teeth
of some Laelius Balbus, a man cruelly eloquent and bloodily
learned. No, what sayest thou, Faunus?   250

HERCULES.

With an undoubted breast thus, I may speak boldly.

HEROD.

By this night I'll speak broadly first and thou wilt, man.
Our Duke of Urbin is a man very happily mad, for he thinks
himself right perfectly wise, and most demonstratively
learned; nay, more—   255

HERCULES.

No more, I'll on. Methinks the young lord our prince of
Ferrara so bounteously adorned with all of grace, feature,
and best-shaped proportion, fair use of speech, full opportunity, and that which makes the sympathy of all, equality
of heat, of years, of blood. Methinks these loadstones 260
should attract the metal of the young princess rather to the
son than to the noisome, cold, and most weak side of his
half-rotten father.

HEROD.

Th'art ours, th'art ours. Now dare we speak as boldly as if
Adam had not fallen, and made us all slaves. Hark ye, the 265
duke is an arrant, doting ass, an ass; and in the knowledge
of my very sense, will turn a foolish animal, for his son will
prove like one of Baal's priests, have all the flesh presented to
the idol his father, but he in the night will feed on't, will
devour it. He will, yeoman of the bottles, he will.   270

HERCULES.

Now gentleman, I am sure the lust of speech hath equally
drenched us all; know I am no servant to this Prince
Tiberio.

HEROD.

Not?

249. Balbus] *Bullen;* Baldus *Q 1–2.*

---

249. *Laelius Balbus*] informer in the days of Tiberius. (Bullen).
251. *undoubted breast*] with confidence in your secrecy.
260. *loadstones*] magnets.
268–270. *prove ... devour it*] the allusion is to the Apocryphal story of
Bel and the Dragon (Dilke).

HERCULES.

Not, but one to him out of some private urging most 275
vowed; one that pursues him but for opportunity of safe
satisfaction. Now if ye can prefer my service to him, I shall
rest yours wholly.

HEROD.

Just in the devil's mouth! Thou shalt have place, Fawn, thou
shalt. Behold this generous Nymphadoro, a gallant of a 280
clean boot, straight back, and beard of a most hopeful
expectation. He is a servant of fair Dulcimel's, her very
creature, born to the princess' sole adoration, a man so
spent in time to her that pity (if no more of grace) must
follow him when we have gained the room, second his suit. 285

HERCULES.

I'll be your intelligencer, your very heart, and if need be
work to most desperate ends.

HEROD.

Well urged.

HERCULES.

Words fit acquaintance, but full actions friends.

NYMPHADORO.

Thou shalt not want, Faunus.   290

HERCULES.

You promise well.

HEROD.

Be thou but firm, that old doting iniquity of age, that oily-
eyed lecherous duke thy lord shall be baffl'd to extremest
derision; his son prove his fool father's own issue.

276. safe] *Q2;* false *Q1.*
281. beard] *Q2;* head *Q1 (cf.*
Marston's Dutch Courtesan,
III.i.63).
285. him] *Q2;* him second *Q1.*
285. second] *Q2;* seru'd *Q1.*
286. HERCULES . . . intelligencer]
Q1–2, 1633, and all modern edns.
print as part of Herod's preceding
speech, with emendation in Bullen and

Wood of Hercules *to* Faunus. *Q1–2*
and subsequent edns. begin Hercules'
speech with Our very heart.
286. your very] *this edn.;* Our very
Q1–2.
292. oily] *J. C. Maxwell,* N&Q
(CCVI, 195), G. Smith, N&Q
(CCVI, 397); only [?] Q1; only Q2,
Wood; horny Bullen *(cf. IV.i.529).*

---

277. *prefer*] recommend.
289. *Words . . . friends*] proverbial (Taylor, p. 216).
293. *baffl'd*] disgraced.

NYMPHADORO.

And we, and thou with us, blessed and enriched past all 295
misery of possible contempt, and above the hopes of greatest
conjectures.

HERCULES.

Nay, as for wealth, *vilia miretur vulgus.* I know by his
physiognomy, for wealth he is of my addiction, and bids a
fico for't.   300

NYMPHADORO.

Why, thou art but a younger brother, but poor Baldazozo.

HEROD.

Faith, to speak truth, my means are written in the book of
fate, as yet unknown, and yet I am at my fool and my
hunting gelding. Come, *via*, to this feastful entertainment.

Exeunt. Remanet Hercules.

HERCULES.

I never knew till now how old I was.   305
By Him by Whom we are, I think a prince
Whose tender sufferance never felt a gust
Of bolder breathings, but still liv'd gently fann'd
With the soft gales of his own flatterers' lips,
Shall never know his own complexion.   310
Dear sleep and lust, I thank you. But for you,
Mortal till now, I scarce had known myself.
Thou grateful poison, sleek mischief, flattery,
Thou dreamful slumber (that doth fall on kings
As soft and soon as their first holy oil),   315
Be thou forever damn'd. I now repent
Severe indictions to some sharp styles;

---

298. *vilia . . . vulgus*] "Let what is cheap excite the marvel of the crowd"
(Ovid, *Amores*, XV. 36).

300. *fico*] "'To give the fico' was to thrust the thumb between the fore-
fingers or swell out the cheek by putting it into the mouth" (Hertford and
Simpson, *Ben Jonson*, IX, 364).

301. *Baldazozo*] (Baldonzozo) "bolde, saucie, presumptuous" (Florio,
p. 52).

304. *via*] come.

311–312. *Dear . . . myself*] "Alexander said, that he knew himselfe
mortall chiefly by this action [the sexual act], and by sleeping" (Montaigne,
III, v, 792).

Freeness, so't grow not to licentiousness,
Is grateful to just states. Most spotless kingdom,
And men, O happy born under good stars,   320
Where what is honest you may freely think,
Speak what you think, and write what you do speak,
Not bound to servile soothings. But since our rank
Hath ever been afflicted with these flies
(That blow corruption on the sweetest virtues),   325
I will revenge us all upon you all
With the same stratagem we still are caught,
Flattery itself; and sure all knows the sharpness
Of reprehensive language is even blunted
To full contempt. Since vice is now term'd fashion,   330
And most are grown to ill even with defense,
I vow to waste this most prodigious heat,
That falls into my age like scorching flames
In depth of numb'd December, in flattering all
In all of their extremest viciousness,   335
Till in their own lov'd race they fall most lame,
And meet full butt the close of vice's shame.   *Exit.*

[II.i]
[*Enter*] Herod *and* Nymphadoro *with napkins in their hands, followed
by pages with stools and meat.*

HEROD.

Come, sir, a stool, boy. These court feasts are to us servitors,
court fasts. Such scambling, such shift for to eat, and
where to eat. Here a squire of low degree hath got the carcass
of a plover; there pages of the chamber divide the spoils of
a tatter'd pheasant; here the sewer has friended a country   5
gentleman with a sweet green goose, and there a young

---

327. *still*] continually.   331. *even with*] despite.
337. *full butt*] head on.
[II.i]
   1. *servitors*] waiters.
   2. *scambling*] scrambling.
   2. *shift*] contrivance.
   5. *sewer*] principal waiter, who also seated the guests.

fellow that late has bought his office, has caught a woodcock by the nose, "with cups full ever flowing."

NYMPHADORO.

But is not Faunus preferr'd with a right hand?

HEROD.

Did you ever see a fellow so spurted up in a moment? He　10
has got the right ear of the duke, the prince, princess,
most of the lords, but all the ladies; why, he is become their
only minion, usher, and supporter.

NYMPHADORO.

He hath gotten more lov'd reputation of virtue, of learning,
of all graces, in one hour, than all your snarling reformers　15
have in—

HEROD.

Nay, that's unquestionable, and indeed what a fruitless
labor, what a filling of Danae's tub, is it become to inveigh
against folly! Community takes away the sense, and
example the shame. No, praise me these fellows, hang on　20
their chariot wheel,
And mount with them whom fortune heaves, nay drives;
A stoical sour virtue seldom thrives.
Oppose such fortune, and then burst with those are pitied.
The hill of chance is pav'd with poor men's bones,　25
And bulks of luckless souls, over whose eyes
Their chariot wheels must ruthless grate, that rise.

Enter Hercules *freshly suited.*

NYMPHADORO.

Behold that thing of most fortunate, most prosperous
impudence, Don Faunus himself.

HEROD.

Blessed and long lasting be thy carnation ribbon, O man　30

25–27. The . . . rise] *Q2; not in Q1.*　29. impudence] *Q2; not in Q1.*

13. *minion*] favorite.
13. *usher*] chamberlain.
18. *Danae's tub*] the daughters of Danaus (the Danaides) were punished
for murder by being condemned to an eternal pouring of water into a
vessel with holes in its bottom.
26. *bulks*] bodies.
30. *carnation ribbon*] bright, courtly dress. Cf. *Love's Labour's Lost,* III.i.146.

of more than wit, much more than virtue, of fortune!
Faunus, wilt eat any of a young spring sallet?

HERCULES.

Where did the herbs grow, my gallant, where did they
grow?

HEROD.

Hard by in the city here. 35

HERCULES.

No, I'll none. I'll eat no city herbs, no city roots, for here in
the city a man shall have his excrements in his teeth again
within four and twenty hours. I love no city sallets. Hast
any canary?

NYMPHADORO.

How the poor snake wriggles with this sudden warmth. 40

Herod *drinks*.

HEROD.

Here, Faunus, a health as deep as a female.

HERCULES.

'Fore Jove, we must be more endear'd.

NYMPHADORO.

How dost thou feel thyself now, Fawn?

HERCULES.

Very womanly, with my fingers. I protest I think I shall
love you. Are you married? I am truly taken with your 45
virtues. Are you married?

HEROD.

Yes.

HERCULES.

Why, I like you well for it.

HEROD.

No, troth, Fawn, I am not married.

HERCULES.

Why, I like you better for it; 'fore heaven, I must love you. 50

---

32. Faunus] *Q2; not in Q1.*   40. snake] *Q2;* snayle *Q1.*

32. *sallet*] salad.
39. *canary*] light, sweet wine from the Canary Islands.

HEROD.

Why, Fawn, why?

HERCULES.

'Fore heaven you are blest with three rare graces: fine linen, clean linings, a sanguine complexion, and I am sure, an excellent wit, for you are a gentleman born.

HEROD.

Thank thee, sweet Fawn, but why is clean linen such a grace,   55
I prithee?

HERCULES.

O my excellent and inward dearly approved friend—What's your name, sir? Clean linen is the first our life craves, and the last our death enjoys.

HEROD.

But what hope rests for Nymphadoro? Thou art now   60
within the buttons of the prince. Shall the duke his father marry the lady?

HERCULES.

'Tis to be hoped, not.

NYMPHADORO.

That's some relief as long as there's hope.

HERCULES.

But sure, sir, 'tis almost undoubted the lady will carry him.   65

NYMPHADORO.

O pestilent air, is there no plot so cunning, no surmise so false, no way of avoidance?

HERCULES.

Hast thou any pity, either of his passion or the lady's years? A gentleman in the summer and hunting season of his youth, the lady met in the same warmth; wer't not to be   70
wept that such a sapless, chafing-dish-using old dotard as the Duke of Ferrara with his withered hand should pluck such a bud, such a—O, the life of sense!

NYMPHADORO.

Thou art now a perfect courtier of just fashion; good grace, canst not relieve us?   75

7 0. his] _Q1;_ hir _Q2._

61. _within the buttons of_] intimate with.
65. _carry_] win.

HERCULES.

Ha' ye any money?

NYMPHADORO.

Pish, Fawn, we are young gallants.

HERCULES.

The liker to have no money. But my young gallants, to
speak like myself, I must hug your humor. Why look you,
there is fate, destiny, constellations, and planets (which 80
though they are under nature, yet they are above women).
Who hath read the book of chance? No, cherish your hope,
sweeten your imaginations with thoughts of—ah, why,
women are the most giddy, uncertain motions under
heaven; 'tis neither proportion of body, virtue of mind, 85
amplitude of fortune, greatness of blood, but only mere
chanceful appetite sways them; which makes some one
like a man, be it but for the paring of his nails. *Via*! As for
inequality, art not a gentleman?

NYMPHADORO.

That I am, and my beneficence shall show it. 90

HERCULES.

I know you are, by that only word beneficence, which only
speaks of the future tense ("shall" know it); but may I
breathe in your bosoms? I only fear Tiberio will abuse his
father's trust, and so make your hopes desperate.

NYMPHADORO.

How? the prince? Would he only stood cross to my wishes, 95
he should find me an Italian.

HERCULES.

How, an Italian?

HEROD.

By thy aid, an Italian. Dear Faunus, thou art now wriggled
into the prince's bosom, and thy sweet hand should
minister that nectar to him, should make him immortal. 100
Nymphadoro, in direct phrase, thou shouldst murder the
prince, so revenge thine own wrongs, and be rewarded for
that revenge.

91. that] *Q1;* the *Q2.*   93. his] *Q1;* your *Q2.*

96. *Italian*] poisoner (Wood).

HERCULES.

Afore the light of my eyes, I think I shall admire, wonder
at you. What? Ha' ye plots, projects, correspondences, and 105
stratagems? Why are not you in better place?

Enter Sir Amoroso.

Who's this?

HEROD.

My eldest brother, Sir Amoroso Debile-Dosso.

HERCULES.

O, I know him. God bless thine eyes, sweet Sir Amoroso, a
rouse, a *vin de monte*, to the health of thy chine, my dear 110
sweet signior.

SIR AMOROSO.

Pardon me, sir. I drink no wine this spring.

HEROD.

O no, sir; he takes the diet this spring always. Boy, my
brother's bottle.

SIR AMOROSO.

Faith, Fawn, an odd unwholesome cold makes me still 115
hoarse and rheumatic.

HEROD.

Yes, in troth, a paltry murr. Last morning he blew nine
bones out of his nose with an odd unwholesome murr. How
does my sister, your lady? What, does she breed?

HERCULES.

I perceive, knight, you have children. O, 'tis a blessed 120
assurance of heaven's favor, and long-lasting name, to
have many children.

SIR AMOROSO.

But I ha' none, Fawn, now.

110. to the health . . . chine] *Q2;* to   112. Pardon . . . spring] *Q1; not in*
health . . . chin *Q1;* to-th health   *Q2.*
. . . chin *1633.*

---

110. *rouse*] carouse.
110. *vin de monte*] (vino del monte) "the best wine in Italie" (Florio, p.
602).
110. *chine*] backbone.
117. *murr*] "a severe form of catarrh" (*OED*); Marston identifies it
with a bone ache, a venereal infection (Wood).
119. *sister*] sister-in-law.

HERCULES.

O, that's most excellent, a right special happiness; he shall
not be a drudge to his cradle, a slave to his child. He 125
shall be sure not to cherish another's blood, nor toil to
advance peradventure some rascal's lust. Without children
a man is unclogg'd, his wife almost a maid. Messalina, thou
criedst out, "O blessed barrenness." Why, once with child,
the very Venus of a lady's entertainment hath lost all 130
pleasure.

SIR AMOROSO.

By this ring, Faunus, I do hug thee with most passionate
affection, and shall make my wife thank thee.

HEROD.

Nay, my brother grudgeth not at my probable inheritance.
He means once to give a younger brother hope to see 135
fortune.

NYMPHADORO.

And yet I hear, Sir Amoroso, you cherish your loins with
high art, the only ingrosser of eringoes, prepar'd cantharides,
cullesses made of dissolved pearl and bruis'd amber; the
pith of parkets and candied lambstones are his perpetual 140
meats. Beds made of the down under pigeons' wings and
goose necks, fomentations, baths, electuaries, frictions, and
all the nurses of most forcible excited concupiscence, he
useth with most nice and tender industry.

HERCULES.

Pish, zoccoli. No, Nymphadoro, if Sir Amorous would ha' 145

---

145. zoccoli] *Q1; Zuccoli Q2.*

---

128. *Messalina*] wife of the emperor Claudius, notorious for her licentiousness.

138. *eringoes . . . cantharides*] aphrodisiacs, candied root of sea holly
(Wood) and Spanish flies, respectively.

139. *cullesses*] meat broths.

140. *parkets*] parakeets.

140. *lambstones*] like the other items, an aphrodisiac.

142. *fomentations*] applications of hot flannels.

142. *electuaries*] medicinal powders mixed with honey, jam or syrup
(*OED*).

142. *frictions*] rubbings.

145. *zoccoli*] "*Zoccoli, Zoccoli*, as we say in mockery, Tush-tush, away, in
faith Sir no" (Florio, p. 616).

children, let him lie on a mattress, plow or thresh, eat
onions, garlic, and leek porridge. Pharaoh and his council
were mistaken, and their device to hinder the increase of
procreation in the Israelites, with enforcing them to much
labor of body, and to feed hard with beets, garlic, and 150
onions (meat that make the original of man most sharp and
taking), was absurd. No, he should have given barley bread,
lettuce, melons, cucumbers, huge store of veal, and fresh
beef, blown up their flesh, held them from exercise, roll'd
them in feathers, and most severely seen them drunk once 155
a day. Then would they at their best have begotten but
wenches, and in short time their generation enfeebled to
nothing.

SIR AMOROSO.

O, divine Faunus, where might a man take up forty pound
in a commodity of garlic and onions? Nymphadoro, thine 160
ear.

HERCULES.

Come, what are you fleering at? There's some weakness
in your brother you wrinkle at thus. Come, prithee impart.
What? We are mutually incorporated, turn'd one into
another, brewed together. Come, I believe you are familiar 165
with your sister, and it were known.

HEROD.

Witch, Faunus, witch. Why, how dost dream I live? Is't
fourscore a year, thinkst thou, maintains my geldings,
my pages, foot-cloths, my best feeding, high play, and excellent company? No, 'tis from hence, from hence, I mint 170
some four hundred pound a year.

HERCULES.

Dost thou live like a porter, by thy back, boy?

155. severely] *Q1, 1633;* s.uerely   *Bullen.*
Q2; surely *Bullen.*   172. thy] *Q1;* the *Q2.*
165. brewed] *this edn.;* brued *Q1–2,*

---

151. *original*] seed.
162. *fleering*] mocking.
168. *fourscore*] i.e., pounds.
169. *foot-cloths*] richly ornamented coverings for horses.

HEROD.

As for my weak-rein'd brother, hang him! He has sore shins.
Damn him heteroclite, his brain's perished. His youth
spent his fodder so fast on other's cattle that he now wants 175
for his own winter. I am fain to supply, Fawn, for which
I am supplied.

HERCULES.

Dost thou branch him, boy?

HEROD.

What else, Fawn?

HERCULES.

What else? Nay, 'tis enough. Why, many men corrupt 180
other men's wives, some their maids, others their neighbors'
daughters, but to lie with one's brother's wedlock, O, my
dear Herod, 'tis vile and uncommon lust.

HEROD.

'Fore heaven, I love thee to the heart. Well, I may praise
God for my brother's weakness, for I assure thee, the land 185
shall descend to me, my little Fawn.

HERCULES.

To thee, my little Herod? O, my rare rascal, I do find
more and more in thee to wonder at, for thou art indeed—
if I prosper, thou shalt know what. Who's this?

Enter Don Zuccone.

HEROD.

What? Know you not Don Zuccone, the only desperately 190
railing lord at's lady that ever was confidently melancholy;
that egregious idiot, that husband of the most witty, fair,
and (be it spoken with many men's true grief) most chaste
Lady Zoya? But we have entered into a confederacy of
afflicting him. 195

HERCULES.

Plots ha' you laid? Inductions dangerous?

189. Who's this?] *Q2; not in Q1.*   191. lord] *Q2; not in Q1.*

---

173. *weak-rein'd*] weak-loined.
174. *heteroclite*] deviant.
178. *branch*] cuckold.
196. *Plots . . . dangerous*] cf. *Richard III*, I.i.32.

NYMPHADORO.

A quiet bosom to my sweet Don. Are you going to visit
your lady?

ZUCCONE.

What o'clock is't? Is it past three?

HEROD.

Past four, I assure you, sweet Don.   200

ZUCCONE.

O, then, I may be admitted; her afternoon's private nap
is taken. I shall take her napping. I hear there's one jealous
that I lie with my own wife, and begins to withdraw his
hand. I protest, I vow—and you will, on my knees I'll
take my sacrament on it—I lay not with her this four year, 205
this four year. Let her not be turn'd upon me, I beseech you.

HERCULES.

My dear Don!

ZUCCONE.

O, Faunus, do'st know our lady?

HERCULES.

Your lady?

ZUCCONE.

No, our lady. For the love of charity incorporate with her; 210
I would have all nations and degrees, all ages know our
lady, for I covet only to be undoubtedly notorious.

HERCULES.

For indeed, sir, a repressed fame mounts like camomile,
the more trod down, the more it grows; things known
common and undoubted, lose rumor.   215

NYMPHADORO.

Sir, I hope yet your conjectures may err; your lady keeps
full face, unbated roundness, cheerful aspect. Were she so
infamously prostitute, her cheek would fall, her color fade,
the spirit of her eye would die.

205. her this four] *Q2;* her this
long *Q1.*

---

202. *jealous*] suspicious.
203–204. *withdraw his hand*] lose interest.
213–214. *mounts . . . grows*] proverbial (Tilley C34); perhaps, like
I Henry IV (II.iv.441–442), a parody of Lyly's style.

ZUCCONE.

O, young man, such women are like Danae's tub, and 220
indeed all women are like Achelous, with whom Hercules
wrestling, he was no sooner hurl'd to the earth, but he rose
up with double vigor. Their fall strengtheneth them.

Enter Dondolo.

DONDOLO.

News, news, news, news! O, my dear Don, be rais'd, be
jovial, be triumphant, ah, my dear Don.   225

NYMPHADORO.

To me first in private, thy news, I prithee.

DONDOLO.

Will you be secret?

NYMPHADORO.

O' my life.

DONDOLO.

As you are generous?

NYMPHADORO.

As I am generous.   230

DONDOLO.

Don Zuccone's lady's with child.

HEROD.

Nymph, Nymph, what is't? What's the news?

NYMPHADORO.

You will be secret?

HEROD.

Silence itself.

NYMPHADORO.

Don Zuccone's lady's with child apparently.   235

HERCULES.

Herod, Herod, what's the matter prithee? The news?

223.1. *Enter*] *Q1;* Exit *Q2.*   225. jovial] *1633;* Iouiald *Q1–2.*

220. *Danae's tub*] cf. II.i.18.n.
221. *Achelous*] a river god. His fight with Hercules is described in Ovid's
Metamorphoses, IX. 4 ff. But Marston has confused Achelous with the giant
Antaeus, with whom Hercules also fought, and who, whenever he was
thrown, arose stronger than before from contact with his mother Earth.
235. *apparently*] evidently, obviously.

HEROD.

You must tell nobody.

HERCULES.

As I am generous—

HEROD.

Don Zuccone's lady's with child apparently.

ZUCCONE.

Fawn, what's the whisper? What's the fool's secret news?   240

HERCULES.

Truth, my lord, a thing, that, that—well, i'faith, it is not fit
you know it.

ZUCCONE.

Not fit I know it? As thou art baptiz'd, tell me, tell me.

HERCULES.

Will you plight your patience to it?

ZUCCONE.

Speak, I am a very block. I will not be mov'd. I am a very   245
block.

HERCULES.

But if you should grow disquiet (as I protest, it would make
a saint blaspheme), I should be unwilling to procure your
impatience.

ZUCCONE.

Yes, do, burst me, burst me, burst me with longing.   250

HERCULES.

Nay, faith, 'tis no great matter. Hark ye, you'll tell nobody?

ZUCCONE.

Not.

HERCULES.

As you are noble?

ZUCCONE.

As I am honest.

HERCULES.

Your lady wife is apparently with child.   255

ZUCCONE.

With child?

241. that, that] Q2; that beautie   242. it] Q2; it? now, now, now Q1
Q1.   255. is] Q1; not in Q2.

HERCULES.

    With child.

ZUCCONE.

    Fool!

HERCULES.

    My Don.

ZUCCONE.

    With child! By the pleasure of generation, I proclaim I lay 260
not with her this—give us patience, give us patience—

HERCULES.

    Why? My lord, 'tis nothing to wear a forker.

ZUCCONE.

    Heaven and earth!

HERCULES.

    All things under the moon are subject to their mistress'
grace. Horns! Lend me your ring, my Don. I'll put it on 265
my finger. Now 'tis on yours again. Why, is the gold now ere
the worse in luster or fitness?

ZUCCONE.

    Am I us'd thus?

HERCULES.

    Ay, my lord, true. Nay, to be (look ye, mark ye) to be us'd
like a dead ox, to have your own hide pluck'd on, to be 270
drawn on, with your own horn, to have the lordship of
your father, the honor of your ancestors, maugre your
beard, to descend to the base lust of some groom of your
stable, or the page of your chamber!

ZUCCONE.

    O, Phalaris, thy bull!   275

SIR AMOROSO.

    Good Don, ha' patience. You are not the only cuckold.
I would now be separated.

---

262. forker] *Q2;* forke *Q1.*

    270–271. *pluck'd . . . horn*] stripped. A dead ox's horn was used to strip
the hide from the body; here used with a play on "horn."

    272. *maugre*] in spite of.

    275. *Phalaris*] tyrant of Acragas in Sicily, probably in the first half oₐ
the sixth century B.C. He is said to have roasted his enemies in a brazen
bull.

ZUCCONE.

'Las, that's but the least drop of the storm of my revenge.
I will unlegitimate the issue. What I will do shall be
horrible but to think.   280

HERCULES.

But, sir—

ZUÇCONE.

But sir! I will do what a man of my form may do, and—
laugh on, laugh on, do, Sir Amorous, you have a lady, too.

HEROD.

But, my sweet lord—

ZUCCONE.

Do not anger me, lest I most dreadfully curse thee, and 285
wish thee married. O, Zuccone, spit white, spit thy gall out.
The only boon I crave of heaven is—but to have my
honors inherited by a bastard! I will be most tyrannous,
bloodily tyrannous in my revenge, and most terrible in
my curses. Live to grow blind with lust, senseless with use, 290
loathed after, flattered before, hated always, trusted never,
abhorred ever, and last may she live to wear a foul smock
seven weeks together, heaven, I beseech thee!   *Exit.*

Enter Zoya *and* Poveia.

ZOYA.

Is he gone? Is he blown off? Now, out upon him, un-
sufferably jealous fool.   295

DONDOLO.

Lady—

ZOYA.

Didst thou give him the fam'd report? Does he believe I
am with child? Does he give faith?

DONDOLO.

In most sincerity, most sincerely.

HERCULES.

Nay, 'tis a pure fool. I can tell ye he was bred up in 300
Germany.

279. unlegitimate] *Q2;* vnlegitti-   293.1.] *after l. 295 in Q 1–2.*
mall *Q 1.*

_____

297. *fam'd*] rumored.

NYMPHADORO.

But the laughter rises, that he vows he lay not in your bed
this four year with such exquisite protestations.

ZOYA.

That's most full truth. He hath most unjustly severed his
sheets ever since the old Duke Pietro (heaven rest his soul)— 305

DONDOLO.

Fie, you may not pray for the dead. 'Tis indifferent to them
what you say.

NYMPHADORO.

Well said, fool.

ZOYA.

Ever since the old Duke Pietro, the great devil of hell torture
his soul.— 310

DONDOLO.

O, lady, yet charity!

ZOYA.

Why? 'Tis indifferent to them what you say, fool. But does
my lord ravel out? Does he fret? For pity of an afflicted lady,
load him soundly. Let him not go clear from vexation.
He has the most dishonorably, with the most sinful, most 315
vicious obstinacy, persevered to wrong me that, were I not
of a male constitution, 'twere impossible for me to survive it.
But in madness' name, let him on. I ha' not the weak fence
of some of your soft-eyed whimpering ladies, who, if they
were us'd like me, would gall their fingers with wringing 320
their hands, look like bleeding Lucreces, and shed salt
water enough to powder all the beef in the duke's larder.
No, I am resolute Donna Zoya. Ha, that wives were of
my metal! I would make these ridiculously jealous fools
howl like a starved dog before he got a bit. I was created to 325
be the affliction of such an unsanctified member, and will
boil him in his own syrup.

Enter Zuccone *listening.*

314. go] *Q2;* worke *Q1.*   *Bullen.*
318. fence] *Q1–2, Wood;* sense   323. resolute] *Q2;* resolved *Q1.*

302. *that*] because.
317. *male*] strong.

HERCULES.

Peace, the wolf's ear takes the wind of us.

HEROD.

The enemy is in ambush.

ZOYA.

If any man ha' the wit, now let him talk wantonly, but not 330
bawdily. Come, gallants, who'll be my servants? I am now
very open-hearted, and full of entertainment.

HERCULES.

Grace me to call you mistress.

NYMPHADORO.

Or me.

HEROD.

Or me.   335

SIR AMOROSO.

Or me.

ZOYA.

Or all! I am taken with you all, with you all.

HERCULES.

As indeed, why should any woman only love any one man,
since it is reasonable women should affect all perfection,
but all perfection never rests in one man. Many men have 340
many virtues, but ladies should love many virtues; therefore ladies should love many men. For as in women, so in
men, some woman hath only a good eye, one can discourse
beautifully, if she do not laugh, one's well favored to her
nose, another hath only a good brow, t'other a plump lip, 345
a third only holds beauty to the teeth, and there the soil
alters; some, peradventure, hold good to the breast, and
then downward turn like the dreamt-of image, whose head
was gold, breast silver, thighs iron, and all beneath clay
and earth. One only winks eloquently, another only kisses 350
well, t'other only talks well, a fourth only lies well. So in
men, one gallant has only a good face, another has only a

338. any one man] *Q2;* such an   yea, all should covet many virtues,
one *Q1.*   therefore Ladies should covet many
340–342. but . . . many men] *Q2;*   men *Q1.*

330–331. *wantonly . . . not bawdily*] freely, not lewdly.
348. *image*] cf. Daniel 2:32–34.

grave methodical beard, and is a notable wise fellow, until
he speaks; a third only makes water well, and that's a good
provoking quality; one only swears well, another only 355
speaks well, a third only does well. All in their kind good:
goodness is to be affected, therefore they. It is a base thing,
and indeed an impossible, for a worthy mind to be contented
with the whole world, but most vile and abject to be satis-
fied with one point of the world.   360

ZOYA.

Excellent, Faunus, I kiss thee for this, by this hand.

SIR AMOROSO.

I thought as well; kiss me, too, dear mistress.

ZOYA.

No, good Sir Amorous, your teeth hath taken rust, your
breath wants airing, and indeed I love sound kissing. Come,
gallants, who'll run a caranto, or leap a lavolto?   365

HERCULES.

Take heed, lady, from offending or bruising the hope of
your womb.

ZOYA.

No matter, now I ha' the sleight, or rather the fashion of it,
I fear no barrenness.

HERCULES.

O, but you know not your husband's aptness.   370

ZOYA.

Husband? husband? as if women could have no children
without husbands.

NYMPHADORO.

Ay, but then they will not be so like your husband.

ZOYA.

No matter, they'll be like their father. 'Tis honor enough
to my husband that they vouchsafe to call him father, and 375
that his land shall descend to them. (Does he not gnash
his very teeth in anguish?) Like our husband? I had
rather they were ungroan'd for. Like our husband? Prove

360. point] *Q2;* point or pricke *Q1.*

---

353. *methodical*] neat.
365. *caranto . . . lavolto*] lively dances.

such a melancholy jealous ass as he is? (Does he not
stamp?)   380

NYMPHADORO.

But troth, your husband has a good face.

ZOYA.

Faith, good enough face for a husband. Come, gallants,
I'll dance to mine own whistle: I am as light now as—
Ah! (*She sings and dances.*) A kiss to you, to my sweet
free servants. Dream on me, and adieu.   385

Exit Zoya. Zuccone *discovers himself.*

ZUCCONE.

I shall lose my wits.

HERCULES.

Be comforted, dear Don, you ha' none to lose.

ZUCCONE.

My wife is grown like a Dutch crest, always rampant,
rampant. 'Fore I will endure this affliction, I will live by
raking cockles out of kennels. Nay, I will run my country, 390
forsake my religion, go weave fustians, or roll the wheelbarrow at Rotterdam.

HERCULES.

I would be divorced despite her friends, or the oath of her
chambermaid.

ZUCCONE.

Nay, I will be divorced in despite of 'em all. I'll go to law 395
with her.

HERCULES.

That's excellent; nay, I would go to law.

ZUCCONE.

Nay, I will go to law.

HERCULES.

Why, that's sport alone. What though it be most exacting?
Wherefore is money?   400

ZUCCONE.

True, wherefore is money?

---

388. *rampant*] heraldic term, used of a beast rearing with both forepaws
in the air; high-spirited.
391–392. *roll the wheelbarrow at Rotterdam*] become a Jew? (Wood).
399. *exacting*] expensive.

HERCULES.

What though you shall pay for every quill, each drop of ink,
each minim, letter, tittle, comma, prick, each breath, nay,
not only for thine own orator's prating, but for some other
orator's silence, though thou must buy silence with a full 405
hand. 'Tis well known Demosthenes took above two
thousand pound once only to hold his peace. Though thou
a man of noble gentry, yet you must wait and besiege his
study door, which will prove more hard to be enter'd than
old Troy, for that was gotten into by a wooden horse, but 410
the entrance of this may chance cost thee a whole stock of
cattle, *Oves et boves, et caetera pecora campi*, though then thou
must sit there, thrust and contemned, bareheaded to a gro-
graine scribe, ready to start up at the door creaking, press'd
to get in, "with your leave, sir," to some surly groom, the 415
third son of a ropemaker; what of all this?

ZUCCONE.

To a resolute mind, these torments are not felt.

HERCULES.

A very arrant ass, when he is hungry, will feed on, though he
be whipt to the bones, and shall a very arrant ass be more
virtuously patient than a noble Don?   420

ZUCCONE.

No, Fawn, the world shall know I have more virtue than
so.

HERCULES.

Do so and be wise.

ZUCCONE.

I will, I warrant thee. So I may be revenged, what care I
what I do?   425

HERCULES.

Call a dog worshipful!

---

421. S.P.] *In Q 1–2, Zuccone follows*   *Zuccone "Don," not "Zuccone" (e.g.,*
ass (*l. 419*), *and* Don *is the speech prefix*   *above, l. 387); and the "I" of l. 421.*
to l. 421. But Hercules elsewhere calls   *is clearly Zuccone.*

---

403. *minim . . . tittle . . . prick*] small strokes of a pen in writing.

406. *Demosthenes*] After first advising the Athenians to expel Harpalus,
Demosthenes pretended that he had lost his voice. It was later discovered
that he had been bribed. (Plutarch, pp. 1036–1037.)

412. *Oves . . . campi*] Sheep and cows and other cattle of the fields.

ZUCCONE.

    Nay, I will embrace—nay I will embrace a jakes-farmer
after eleven o'clock at night. I will stand bare and give wall
to a bellows-mender, pawn my lordship, sell my foot-cloth,
but I will be reveng'd. Does she think she has married an   430
ass?

HERCULES.

    A fool?

ZUCCONE.

    A coxcomb?

HERCULES.

    A ninny-hammer?

ZUCCONE.

    A woodcock?   435

HERCULES.

    A calf?

ZUCCONE.

    No, she shall find that I ha' eyes.

HERCULES.

    And brain.

ZUCCONE.

    And nose.

HERCULES.

    And forehead.   440

ZUCCONE.

    She shall, i'faith, Fawn, she shall, she shall, sweet Fawn,
she shall, i'faith, old boy. It joys my blood to think on't.
She shall, i'faith. Farewell, lov'd Fawn, sweet Fawn, farewell. She shall, i'faith, boy.   *Exit* Zuccone.

    Enter Gonzago, *and* Granuffo *with* Dulcimel.

---

  427. *jakes-farmer*] privy cleaner.
  428. *stand bare and give wall*] show respect by removing one's hat and
passing on the street side of a sidewalk.
  429. *foot-cloth*] cf. II.i.169n.
  434. *ninny-hammer*] simpleton.
  435. *woodcock*] easily duped bird.
  440. *forehead*] the site of the cuckold's horns.

GONZAGO.

We would be private; only Faunus stay. 445

Exeunt [*all but* Gonzago, Granuffo, Hercules *and* Dulcimel].

He is a wise fellow, daughter, a very wise fellow, for he is
still just of my opinion. My Lord Granuffo, you may
likewise stay, for I know you'll say nothing. Say on,
daughter.

DULCIMEL.

And as I told you, sir, Tiberio being sent, 450
Grac'd in high trust as to negotiate
His royal father's love, if he neglect
The honor of this faith, just care of state,
And every fortune that gives likelihood
To his best hopes, to draw our weaker heart 455
To his own love (as I protest he does)—

GONZAGO.

I'll rate the prince with such a heat of breath
His ears shall glow. Nay, I discover'd him.
I read his eyes, as I can read an eye,
Though it speak in darkest characters I can. 460
Can we not, Fawn? Can we not, my lord?
Why, I conceive you now, I understand you both.
You both admire, yes, say is't not hit?
Though we are old, or so, yet we ha' wit.

DULCIMEL.

And you may say (if so your wisdom please 465
As you are truly wise) how weak a creature
Soft woman is to bear the siege and strength
Of so prevailing feature and fair language,
As that of his is ever: you may add
(If so your wisdom please, as you are wise)— 470

GONZAGO.

As mortal man may be.

DULCIMEL.

I am of years apt for his love, and if he should proceed

457. rate] *Q2, 1633;* hate *Q1.*

---

457. *rate*] berate.
460. *darkest*] most obscure.
462. *conceive*] understand.

In private urgent suit, how easy 'twere
To win my love, for you may say (if so
Your wisdom please) you find in me   475
A very forward passion to enjoy him.
And therefore you beseech him seriously
Straight to forbear, with such close-cunning art
To urge his too-well-graced suit: for you
(If so your lordship please) may say I told you all.   480

GONZAGO.

Go to, go to, what I will say or so,
Until I say, none but myself shall know.
But I will say, go to; does not my color rise?
It shall rise, for I can force my blood
To come and go, as men of wit and state,   485
Must sometimes feign their love, sometimes their hate.
That's policy now. But come. With this free heat,
Or this same Estro or Enthusiasm
(For these are phrases both poetical),
Will we go rate the prince, and make him see   490
Himself in us; that is, our grace and wits,
Shall show his shapeless folly; vice kneels whiles virtue sits.

Enter Tiberio.

But see, we are prevented. Daughter, in!
It is not fit thyself should hear what I
Must speak of thy most modest, wise, wise mind.   495
For th'art careful, sober, in all most wise

                                    Exit Dulcimel.

And indeed our daughter. My Lord Tiberio,
A horse but yet a colt may leave his trot,
A man but yet a boy may well be broke
From vain addictions. The head of rivers stopp'd,   500
The channel dries. He that doth dread a fire,
Must put out sparks, and he who fears a bull,
Must cut his horns off when he is a calf.
Principiis obsta, saith a learned man

474. so] *Q2; not in Q1.*

---

488. *Estro*] the *Oestrus*, or gadfly; "something that stings or goads one on,
a stimulus" (*OED*).
504. *Principiis obsta*] "Resist beginnings" (Ovid, *Remedia Amoris*, I. 91).

Who, though he was no duke, yet he was wise,   505
And had some sense or so.

TIBERIO.   What means my Lord?

GONZAGO.

La, sir! thus men of brain can speak in clouds
Which weak eyes cannot pierce. But, my fair lord,
In direct phrase, thus: my daughter tells me plain
You go about with most direct entreats   510
To gain her love, and to abuse your father.
O, my fair lord, will you, a youth so blest
With rarest gifts of fortune and sweet graces,
Offer to love a young and tender lady,
Will you I say abuse your most wise father,   515
Who though he freeze in August, and his calves
Are sunk into his toes, yet may well wed our daughter
As old as he in wit? Will you, I say
(For, by my troth, my lord, I must be plain)?
My daughter is but young, and apt to love   520
So fit a person as your proper self,
And so she pray'd me tell you. Will you now
Entice her easy breast to abuse your trust,
Her proper honor, and your father's hopes?
I speak no figures, but I charge you check   525
Your appetite and passions to our daughter
Before it head, nor offer conference
Or seek access but by and before us.
What, judge you us as weak, or as unwise?
No, you shall find that Venice' duke has eyes;   530
And so think on't.   *Exeunt* Gonzago *and* Granuffo.

TIBERIO.

Astonishment and wonder, what means this?
Is the duke sober?

HERCULES.   Why ha' not you endeavor'd
Courses that only seconded appetite,
And not your honor, or your trust of place?   535

---

507. S.P. GONZAGO.] *Q2; not in Q1.*   *l. 515, below*).
511. your] *this edn.;* her *Q1–2 (cf.*   534. only] *Q2;* have *Q1.*

---

525. *figures*] figures of speech.

Do you not court the lady for yourself?

TIBERIO.

 Fawn, thou dost love me. If I ha' done so,
'Tis past my knowledge, and I prithee, Fawn,
If thou observ'st I do I know not what,
Make me to know it, for by the dear light   540
I ha' not found a thought that way. I apt for love?
Let lazy idleness fill'd full of wine,
Heated with meats, high fed with lustful ease,
Go dote on color. As for me, why, death o' sense,
I court the lady? I was not born in Cyprus.   545
I love, when? how? whom? Think, let us yet keep
Our reason sound. I'll think, and think, and sleep. *Exit.*

HERCULES.

 Amaz'd, even lost in wond'ring, I rest full
Of covetous expectation. I am left
As on a rock, from whence I may discern   550
The giddy sea of humor flow beneath,
Upon whose back the vainer bubbles float
And forthwith break. O mighty flattery,
Thou easiest, common'st, and most grateful venom
That poisons courts and all societies,   555
How grateful dost thou make me? Should one rail
And come to fear a vice, beware **leg-rings**
And the turn'd key on thee, when, if softer hand
Suppling a sore that itches (which should smart)—
Free speech gains foes, base fawnings steal the heart. 560
Swell, you impostum'd members, till you burst,
Since 'tis in vain to hinder; on I'll thrust,
And when in shame you fall, I'll laugh from hence,
And cry, "So end all desperate impudence."
Another's court shall show me where and how 565

---

543. Heated] *Q2;* Heau'd *Q1.* 544. death] *Q2;* earth *Q1.*

544. *color*] outward appearance.
545. *Cyprus*] a seat of worship of Aphrodite; therefore a land devoted to the art of love.
551. *humor*] temperament.
557. *to fear*] to frighten.
561. *impostum'd*] abscessed.

Vice may be cur'd; for now beside myself,
Possess'd with almost frenzy, from strong fervor
I know I shall produce things near divine.
Without immoderate heat, no virtues shine.
For I speak strong, though strange: the dews that steep   570
Our souls in deepest thoughts, are fury and sleep.   *Exit.*

[III.i]   *Enter* Hercules *and* Nymphadoro.

NYMPHADORO.

Faith, Faunus, 'tis my humor, the natural sin of my sanguine
complexion. I am most enforcedly in love with all women,
almost affecting them all with an equal flame.

HERCULES.

An excellent justice of an upright virtue. You love all God's
creatures with an unpartial affection.   5

NYMPHADORO.

Right, neither am I inconstant to any one in particular.

HERCULES.

Though you love all in general, true; for when you vow
a most devoted love to one, you swear not to tender a most
devoted love to another, and indeed why should any man
over-love any thing? 'Tis judgment for a man to love every-   10
thing proportionably to his virtue. I love a dog with a
hunting pleasure, as he is pleasurable in hunting; my horse
after a journeying easiness, as he is easy in journeying; my
hawk, to the goodness of his wing, and my wench—

NYMPHADORO.

How, sweet Fawn, how?   15

---

568. near] *this edn.*; meere *Q 1–2*   *in the explanatory note to lines 566–*
(cf. phrase "neerest . . . to divinity"   *571 of present scene).*
in the passage from Montaigne quoted

566–571. *Vice . . . sleep*] ". . . no eminent or glorious vertue, can be
without some immoderate and irregular agitation. . . . Dares not Philosophy
thinke that men produce their greatest effects, and neerest approching to
divinity, when they are beside themselves, furious, and madde? . . . The
two naturall waies, to enter the cabinet of the Gods . . . are furie and sleep"
(Montaigne, II, xii, 512).
[III.i]
    1. *humor . . . sanguine*] according to the physiological theory of the four
bodily humors, a sanguine humor produced an amorous disposition.

HERCULES.

Why, according to her creation. Nature made them pretty, toying, idle, fantastic, imperfect creatures; even so I would in justice affect them, with a pretty, toying, idle, fantastic, imperfect affection; and as indeed they are only created for show and pleasure, so would I only love them for show and   20 pleasure.

NYMPHADORO.

Why, that's my humor to the very thread; thou dost speak my proper thoughts.

HERCULES.

But, sir, with what possibility can your constitution be so boundlessly amorous as to affect all women of what degree,   25 form, or complexion soever?

NYMPHADORO.

I'll tell thee: for mine own part, I am a perfect Ovidian, and can with him affect all. If she be a virgin of a modest eye, shamefac'd, temperate ⌐aspect, her very modesty inflames me, her sober blushes fires me. If I behold a   30 wanton, pretty, courtly, petulant ape, I am extremely in love with her, because she is not clownishly rude, and that she assures her lover of no ignorant, dull, unmoving Venus. Be she sourly severe, I think she wittily counterfeits, and I love her for her wit. If she be learned and censures   35 poets, I love her soul, and for her soul, her body. Be she a lady of profess'd ignorance, O, I am infinitely taken with her simplicity as one assured to find no sophistication about her. Be she slender and lean, she's the Greek's delight. Be she thick and plump, she's the Italian's pleasure.   40 If she be tall, she's of a goodly form, and will print a fair proportion in a large bed. If she be short and low, she's nimbly delightful, and ordinarily quick-witted. Be she young, she's for mine eye. Be she old, she's for my discourse

22. the] *Q2;* a *Q1.*   38. as one] *Q2;* I am *Q1.*
33. unmoving] *Q2;* moving *Q1.*

---

31. *wanton*] frolicsome.
38. *sophistication*] falsification.
41. *print*] imprint.
42. *proportion*] shape.

as one well knowing; there's much amiableness in a grave　45
matron. But be she young or old, lean, fat, short, tall, white,
red, brown, nay, even black, my discourse shall find reason
to love her, if my means may procure opportunity to enjoy
her.

HERCULES.

Excellent, sir. Nay, if a man were of competent means,　50
wer't not a notable delight for a man to have for every
month in the year?

NYMPHADORO.

Nay, for every week of the month?

HERCULES.

Nay, for every day of the week?

NYMPHADORO.

Nay, for every hour of that day?　　　　　　　　　55

HERCULES.

Nay, for every humor of a man in that hour, to have a several
mistress to entertain him, as if he were saturnine, or melancholy, to have a black-haired, pale-fac'd, sallow, thinking
mistress to clip him. If jovial and merry, a sanguine, light-
tripping, singing—indeed a mistress that would dance a　60
caranto as she goes to embrace him. If choleric, impatient,
or ireful, to have a mistress with red hair, little ferret eyes,
a lean cheek, and a sharp nose to entertain him. And so of
the rest.

Enter Donetta.

NYMPHADORO.

O, sir, this were too great ambition. Well I love and am　65
beloved of a great many, for I court all in the way of honor,
in the trade of marriage, Fawn, but above all I affect the
Princess. She's my utmost end. O, I love a lady whose
beauty is joined with fortune, beyond all, yet one of beauty
without fortune for some uses, nay one of fortune without　70
beauty for some ends, but never any that has neither

60. a] *Q2;* and *Q1.*

---

47. *discourse*] power of reasoning.
59. *clip*] embrace.

fortune nor beauty but for necessity. Such a one as this is
Donna Donetta. Here's one has loved all the court just
once over.

HERCULES.

O, this is the fair lady with the foul teeth. Nature's hand 75
shook when she was in making, for the red that should
have spread her cheeks, nature let fall upon her nose; the
white of her skin slipp'd into her eyes, and the gray of her
eyes leapt before his time into her hair; and the yellowness
of her hair fell without providence into her teeth. 80

NYMPHADORO.

By the vow of my heart, you are my most only elected;
and I speak by way of protestation, I shall no longer wish
to be, than that your only affection shall rest in me, and
mine only in you.

DONETTA.

But if you shall love any other? 85

NYMPHADORO.

Any other? Can any man love any other that knows you,
the only perfection of your sex, and astonishment of
mankind?

DONETTA.

Fie, ye flatter me. Go wear and understand my favor, this
snail: slow, but sure. 90

NYMPHADORO.

This kiss.

DONETTA.

Farewell.

NYMPHADORO.

The integrity and only vow of my faith to you, ever urge
your well deserved requital to me. *Exit* Donetta.

HERCULES.

Excellent. 95

NYMPHADORO.

See, here's another of—

78. skin] *Q1, 1633;* chin *Q2.*
89. flatter me] *Q2;* flatterer *Q1;*
flatter *1633.*
92.] *After* Farewell *Q2 prints S.D.*
Exit.
93. urge] *Q2;* vrged *Q1.*

81. *elected*] chosen one.

Enter Garbetza.

HERCULES.

Of your most only elected.

NYMPHADORO.

Right, Donna Garbetza.

HERCULES.

O, I will acknowledge this is the lady made of cutwork, and all her body like a sand box, full of holes, and contains 100 nothing but dust. She chooseth her servants as men choose dogs, by the mouth; if they open well and full, their cry is pleasing. She may be chaste, for she has a bad face, and yet questionless, she may be made a strumpet, for she is covetous.   105

NYMPHADORO.

By the vow of my heart, you are my most only elected; and I speak it by way of protestation, I shall no longer wish to be, than all your affections shall only rest in me, and all mine only in you.

HERCULES.

Excellent. This piece of stuff is good on both sides. He is so 110 constant, he will not change his phrase.

GARBETZA.

But shall I give faith? May you not love another?

NYMPHADORO.

Another? Can any man love another that knows you, the only perfection of your sex, and admiration of mankind?

GARBETZA.

Your speech flies too high for your meaning to follow, yet 115 my mistrust shall not precede my experience. I wrought this favor for you.

NYMPHADORO.

The integrity and only vow of my faith to you, ever urge

118. urge] *this edn.;* vrgde *Q1–2;*
urg'd *1633.*

---

99. *cutwork*] openwork embroidery.
100. *sand box*] box with holes in top, used for drying ink by sprinkling sand.
110. *stuff*] cloth.

your well deserv'd requital to me.   *Exit* Garbetza.

HERCULES.

Why, this is pure wit, nay, judgment.   120

NYMPHADORO.

Why, look thee, Fawn, observe me.

HERCULES.

I do, sir.

NYMPHADORO.

I do love at this instant some nineteen ladies all in the trade of marriage. Now sir, whose father dies first, or whose portion appeareth most, or whose fortunes betters soonest, 125 her with quiet liberty at my leisure will I elect, for that's my humor.

Enter Dulcimel *and* Philocalia.

HERCULES.

You profess a most excellent mystery, sir.

NYMPHADORO.

'Fore heaven, see the princess, she that is—

HERCULES.

Your most only elected, too.   130

NYMPHADORO.

O, ay, O, ay, but my hope's faint yet. —By the vow of my heart, you are my most only elected and—

DULCIMEL.

There's a ship of fools going out. Shall I prefer thee, Nymphadoro? Thou mayst be master's mate. My father hath made Dondolo captain, else thou shouldst have his 135 place.

NYMPHADORO.

By Jove, Fawn, she speaks as sharply and looks as sourly as if she had been new squeezed out of a crab orange.

119. S.D.] *Q2; not in Q1.*   my humour love *Q1.*
126–127. that's my humor] *Q2;* if   138. orange] *Q2; not in Q1.*

127. *humor*] whim.
128. *mystery*] art, craft.
133. *prefer*] recommend.
134. *master's mate*] first mate, second in command.
138. *crab orange*] crab apple (see Tilley C783).

HERCULES.

How term you that lady with whom she holds discourse?

NYMPHADORO.

O, Fawn, 'tis a lady even above ambition, and like the 140
vertical sun, that neither forceth others to cast shadows,
nor can others force or shade her. Her style is Donna
Philocalia.

HERCULES.

Philocalia! What, that renowned lady whose ample report
hath struck wonder into remotest strangers, and yet her 145
worth above that wonder? She whose noble industries
hath made her breast rich in true glories, and undying
habilities? She that whilst other ladies spend the life of
earth, Time, in reading their glass, their jewels, and (the
shame of poesy) lustful sonnets, gives her soul meditations, 150
those meditations wings that cleave the air, fan bright
celestial fires, whose true reflections makes her see herself
and them? She whose pity is ever above her envy, loving
nothing less than insolent prosperity, and pitying nothing
more than virtue destitute of fortune.   155

NYMPHADORO.

There were a lady for Ferrara's duke: one of great blood,
firm age, undoubted honor, above her sex, most modestly
artful, though naturally modest, too excellent to be left
unmatch'd, though few worthy to match with her.

HERCULES.

I cannot tell—my thoughts grow busy.   160

PHILOCALIA.

The princess would be private. Void the presence.

Exeunt [*all but* Dulcimel *and* Philocalia].

DULCIMEL.

May I rest sure thou wilt conceal a secret?

PHILOCALIA.

Yes, madam.

DULCIMEL.

How may I rest truly assur'd?

---

141. *vertical*] directly overhead.
146. *wonder*] admiration.
148. *habilities*] abilities.

PHILOCALIA.

Truly thus: do not tell it me.   165

DULCIMEL.

Why, canst thou not conceal a secret?

PHILOCALIA.

Yes, as long as it is a secret. But when two know it, how
can it be a secret? And indeed with what justice can you
expect secrecy in me that cannot be private to yourself?

DULCIMEL.

Faith, Philocalia, I must of force trust thy silence, for my 170
breast breaks if I confer not my thoughts upon thee.

PHILOCALIA.

You may trust my silence. I can command that. But if I
chance to be questioned I must speak truth. I can conceal
but not deny my knowledge. That must command me.

DULCIMEL.

Fie on these philosophical discoursing women! Prithee 175
confer with me like a creature made of flesh and blood,
and tell me if it be not a scandal to the soul of all being,
proportion, that I, a female of fifteen, of a lightsome and
civil discretion, healthy, lusty, vigorous, full, and idle,
should forever be shackled to the crampy shins of a 180
wayward, dull, sour, austere, rough, rheumy, threescore and
four.

PHILOCALIA.

Nay, threescore and ten at the least.

DULCIMEL.

Now, heaven bless me, as it is pity that every knave is not
a fool, so it is shame that every old man is not and resteth not 185
a widower. They say in China, when women are past child-
bearing, they are all burnt to make gunpowder. I wonder
what men should be done withal, when they are past
child-getting? Yet, upon my love, Philocalia (which with
ladies is often above their honor), I do even dote upon the 190
best part of the duke.

173. be] *Q1;* he *Q 2.*   178. fifteen] *Q2;* 13 *Q1.*

173–174. *I can . . . knowledge*] Cf. Montaigne, III, v, 761: "... my knowledge. I can conceal it; but deny it I cannot."
185. *resteth*] remains.

PHILOCALIA.
What's that?

DULCIMEL.
His son, yes, sooth, and so love him, that I must marry him.

PHILOCALIA.
And wherefore love him, so to marry him?

DULCIMEL.
Because I love him. And because he is virtuous, I love to 195
marry—

PHILOCALIA.
His virtues?

DULCIMEL.
Ay, with him his virtues.

PHILOCALIA.
Ay, with him. Alas, sweet princess, love or virtue are not
of the essence of marriage.   200

DULCIMEL.
A jest upon your understanding! I'll maintain that wisdom
in a woman is most foolish quality. A lady of a good
complexion, naturally well witted, perfectly bred, and well
exercised in discourse of the best men, shall make fools of a
thousand of these book-thinking creatures. I speak it by way 205
of justification. I tell thee—look that nobody eavesdrop us—
I tell thee I am truly learned, for I protest ignorance; and
wise, for I love myself; and virtuous enough for a lady of
fifteen.

PHILOCALIA.
How virtuous?   210

DULCIMEL.
Shall I speak like a creature of a good healthful blood, and
not like one of these weak, green sickness, lean phthisic

195. is] *Q1;* his *Q2.*   207. protest] *Q1;* prote *Q2.*
201. A jest] *Q2;* I iest *Q1;* I rest   207. ignorance] *Q2;* ignorant *Q1.*
1633.

212. *green sickness*] "an anemic disease which most affects young women
about the age of puberty" (*OED*).

starvelings? First for the virtue of magnanimity, I am very
valiant, for there is no heroic action so particularly noble
and glorious to our sex as not to fall to action. The greatest 215
deed we can do is not to do (look that nobody listen).
Then am I full of patience, and can bear more than a
sumpter-horse, for (to speak sensibly) what burden is there
so heavy to a porter's back as virginity to a well-
complexioned young lady's thoughts? (Look nobody 220
harken.) By this hand, the noblest vow is that of virginity,
because the hardest. I will have the prince.

PHILOCALIA.
But by what means, sweet madam?

DULCIMEL.
O, Philocalia, in heavy sadness and unwanton phrase,
there lies all the brain work. By what means? I could fall 225
into a miserable blank verse presently.

PHILOCALIA.
But, dear madam, your reason of loving him?

DULCIMEL.
Faith, only a woman's reason: because I was expressly
forbidden to love him, at the first view I lik'd him, and no
sooner had my father's wisdom mistrusted my liking, but 230
I grew loath his judgment should err. I pitied he should
prove a fool in his old age, and without cause mistrust me.

PHILOCALIA.
But when you saw no means of manifesting your affection to
him, why did not your hopes perish?

DULCIMEL.
O, Philocalia, that difficulty only inflames me. When the 235
enterprise is easy, the victory is inglorious. No, let my wise,
aged, learned, intelligent father, that can interpret eyes,
understand the language of birds, interpret the grumbling

214–216. *heroic . . . to do*] "There is no point of doing more thorny, nor
more active, then this of not doing. I find it easier, to beare all ones life a
combersome armour on his backe, then a maiden-head. And the vow of
virginity, is the noblest of all vows, because the hardest . . . saith St. Jerome"
(Montaigne, III, v, 776).
218. *sumpter-horse*] pack-horse.   230. *mistrusted*] suspected.

of dogs and the conference of cats, that can read even
silence, let him forbid all interviews, all speeches, all 240
tokens, all messages, all (as he thinks) human means. I
will speak to the prince, court the prince that he shall
understand me. Nay, I will so stalk on the blind side of my
all-knowing father's wit that, do what his wisdom can, he
shall be my only mediator, my only messenger, my only 245
honorable spokesman. He shall carry my favors, he shall
amplify my affection. Nay, he shall direct the prince the
means, the very way to my bed, he and only he. When he
only can do this, and only would not do this, he only shall
do this.   250

PHILOCALIA.

Only you shall then deserve such a husband. O, love, how
violent are thy passages!

DULCIMEL.

Pish, Philocalia, 'tis against the nature of love not to be
violent.

PHILOCALIA.

And against the condition of violence to be constant.   255

DULCIMEL.

Constancy? Constancy and patience are virtues in no
living creatures but sentinels and anglers. Here's our
father.

Enter Gonzago, Hercules *and* Granuffo.

GONZAGO.

What, did he think to walk invisibly before our eyes? And
he had Gyges' ring, I would find him.   260

HERCULES.

'Fore Jove, you rated him with emphasis.

GONZAGO.

Did we not shake the prince with energy?

HERCULES.

With Ciceronian elocution!

253–255. *love . . . constant*] ". . . it is against the nature of love, not to be
violent, and against the condition of violence, to be constant" (Montaigne,
III, v, 776).
260. *Gyges' ring*] reputed to confer invisibility.
261. *rated*] berated.

GONZAGO.

And most pathetic piercing oratory?

HERCULES.

If he have any wit in him, he will make sweet use of it.   265

GONZAGO.

Nay, he shall make sweet use of it ere I have done. Lord, what overweening fools these young men be, that think us old men sots.

HERCULES.

Arrant asses.

GONZAGO.

Doting idiots, when we, God wot—ha, ha; 'las, silly souls! 270

HERCULES.

Poor weak creatures to men of approved reach.

GONZAGO.

Full years.

HERCULES.

Of wise experience.

GONZAGO.

And approved wit.

HERCULES.

Nay, as for your wit—   275

GONZAGO.

Count Granuffo, as I live, this Faunus is a rare understander of men, is 'a not? Faunus, this Granuffo is a right wise good lord, a man of excellent discourse, and never speaks. His signs to me, and men of profound reach, instruct abundantly. He begs suits with signs, gives thanks 280 with signs, puts off his hat leisurely, maintains his beard learnedly, keeps his lust privately, makes a nodding leg courtly, and lives happily.

HERCULES.

Silence is an excellent modest grace, but especially before so instructing a wisdom as that of your excellency's. As 285 for his advancement, you gave it most royally, because he

---

270. *wot*] knows.
271. *reach*] penetration.
274. *wit*] knowledge.
282. *nodding leg*] bow.

deserves it least duly, since to give to virtuous desert is
rather a due requital than a princely magnificence, when
to undeservingness it is merely all bounty and free grace.

GONZAGO.

Well spoke, 'tis enough. Don Granuffo, this Faunus is a 290
very worthy fellow, and an excellent courtier, and belov'd
of most of the princes of Christendom, I can tell you; for
howsoever some severer dissembler grace him not when he
affronts him in the full face, yet if he comes behind or on
the one side, he'll leer and put back his head upon him, be 295
sure. Be you two precious to each other.

HERCULES.

Sir, myself, my family, my fortunes, are all devoted, I
protest most religiously, to your service. I vow my whole
self only proud in being acknowledged by you, but as your
creature, and my only utmost ambition is by my sword or 300
soul to testify how sincerely I am consecrated to your
adoration.

GONZAGO.

'Tis enough. Art a gentleman, Fawn?

HERCULES.

Not uneminently descended; for were the pedigrees of some
fortunately mounted, searched, they would be secretly found 305
to be of the blood of the poor Fawn.

GONZAGO.

'Tis enough. You two I love heartily, for thy silence never
displeaseth me, nor thy speech ever offend me. See, our
daughter attends us. —My fair, my wise, my chaste, my
duteous, and indeed, in all my daughter (for such a pretty 310
soul for all the world have I been). What, I think we have
made the prince to feel his error.

What, did he think he had weak fools in hand?

No, he shall find, as wisely said Lucullus,

Young men are fools that go about to gull us.   315

304. uneminently] *Q1;* on-
eminently *Q2.*

---

288. *magnificence*] munificence.

300. *creature*] "One who owes his position to another" (*OED*).

314. *Lucullus*] Roman general and statesman, and the owner of a famous
library (*c.* 114–57 B.C.).

DULCIMEL.

But sooth, my wisest father, the young prince is yet forgetful,
and resteth resolute in his much unadvised love.

GONZAGO.

Is't possible?

DULCIMEL.

Nay, I protest, whate'er he feign to you (as he can feign most
deeply)—   320

GONZAGO.

Right, we know it; for if you mark'd, he would not once
take sense of any such intent from him. O, impudence,
what mercy canst thou look for!

DULCIMEL.

And as I said, royally wise and wisely royal father—

GONZAGO.

I think that eloquence is hereditary.   325

DULCIMEL.

Though he can feign, yet I presume your sense is quick
enough to find him.

GONZAGO.

Quick, is't not, Granuffo? Is't not, Fawn? Why I did know
you feigned, nay I do know (by the just sequence of such
impudence) that he hath laid some second siege unto thy   330
bosom, with most miraculous conveyances of some rich
present to thee.

DULCIMEL.

O bounteous heaven, how liberal are your graces to my
Nestor-like father!

GONZAGO.

Is't not so, say!   335

DULCIMEL.

'Tis so, oraclous father.
He hath now more than courted with bare phrases.
See, father, see, the very bane of honor,
Corruption of justice and virginity,

328. Granuffo] *printed as S.P.* Gra.   332. to] *Q1;* on *Q2.*
in *Q1–2.*

---

334. *Nestor*] aged Greek hero in the Trojan War, noted for his eloquence,
justice, and garrulity.

Gifts, hath he left with me. O view this scarf.   340
This, as he call'd it, most envied silk,
That should embrace an arm, or waist, or side,
Which he much fear'd should never—this he left,
Despite my much resistance.

GONZAGO.

Did he so? Giv't me. I'll giv't him. I'll re-give his token 345
with so sharp advantage.

DULCIMEL.

Nay, my worthy father, read but these cunning letters.

GONZAGO.

Letters! Where? [*Reads*]
"Prove you but justly loving and conceive me,
Till justice leave the gods, I'll never leave thee.   350
For though the duke seem wise, he'll find this strain,
Where two hearts yield consent, all thwarting's vain."
—And darst thou then aver this wicked writ?
O world of wenching wiles, where is thy wit?

                    Enter Tiberio.

DULCIMEL.

But other talk for us were far more fit,   355
For see, here comes the prince Tiberio.

GONZAGO.

Daughter, upon thy obedience, instantly take thy chamber.

DULCIMEL.

Dear father, in all duty, let me beseech your leave, that I
may but—

GONZAGO.

Go to, go to, you are a simple fool, a very simple animal. 360

DULCIMEL.

Yet let me (the loyal servant of simplicity)—

GONZAGO.

What would you do? What, are you wiser than your father?
Will you direct me?

DULCIMEL.

Heavens forbid such insolence, yet let me denounce my
hearty hatred.   365

---

352. yield] *Q2;* finde *Q1.*   361. me] *Q2;* me be *Q1.*
353. wicked] *Q2; not in Q1.*

GONZAGO.

To what end?

DULCIMEL.

Though't be but in the prince's ear (since fits not maiden's
blush to rail aloud)—

GONZAGO.

Go to, go to!

DULCIMEL.

Let me but check his heat.   370

GONZAGO.

Well, well—

DULCIMEL.

And take him down, dear father, from his full pride of
hopes.

GONZAGO.

So, so, I say once more, go in. *Exeunt* Dulcimel *and* Philocalia.
I will not lose the glory of reproof.   375
Is this th' office of ambassadors, my lord Tiberio?
Nay, duty of a son; nay, piety of a man?
(A figure call'd in art *gradatio*:
With some learn'd, *climax*)—to court a royal lady,
For's master, father, or perchance his friend,   380
And yet intend the purchase of such beauty,
To his own use?

TIBERIO.   Your Grace doth much amaze me.

GONZAGO.

Ay, feign, dissemble. 'Las, we are now grown old,
Weak-sighted. Alas, anyone fools us.

TIBERIO.

I deeply vow, my lord—   385

GONZAGO.

Peace, be not damn'd; have pity on your soul.
I confess, sweet prince, for you to love my daughter,
Young and witty, of equal mixture both of mind and body,

370. but] *Q2; not in Q1.*   379. With] *Q2, 1633;* which *Q1.*
374. S.D. *Exeunt*] *Bullen; Exit Q1–2.*   381. such] *Q1;* his *Q2.*
377. piety] *Q1;* pittie *Q2.*

378–379. *gradatio . . . climax*] "*Gradation,* which the Greeks call *climax* . . .
involves *addition,* since it repeats what has already been said and, before
passing to a new point, dwells on those which precede" (Quintilian, *Institutio
Oratoria,* IX, iii, 54–55).

Is neither wondrous nor unnatural.
Yet to forswear and vow against one's heart,   390
Is full of base, ignoble cowardice,
Since 'tis most plain, such speeches do contemn
Heaven, and fear men (that's sententious now).

TIBERIO.
My gracious lord, if I unknowingly have err'd—

GONZAGO.
Unknowingly? Can you blush, my lord?   395
Unknowingly? Why, can you write these lines,
Present this scarf, unknowingly, my lord,
To my dear daughter? Um, unknowingly?
Can you urge your suit, prefer your gentlest love,
In your own right, to her too easy breast   400
That, God knows, takes too much compassion on ye
(And so she pray'd me say), unknowingly, my lord!
If you can act these things unknowingly,
Know we can know your actions so unknown,
For we are old, I will not say in wit   405
(For even just worth must not approve itself);
But take your scarf, for she vows she'll not wear it.

TIBERIO.
Nay, but my lord—

GONZAGO.   Nay, but my lord, my lord,
You must take it, wear it, keep it,
For by the honor of our house and blood,   410
I will deal wisely, and be provident.
Your father shall not say I panderiz'd,
Or fondly wink'd at your affection.

393. sententious] *Q1;* sentious *Q2.*   406. even] *Q2;* euery *Q1.*

390–393. *Yet ... now*] "... whosoever lieth, witnesseth that he con-
temneth God and therewithall feareth men. ... For, what can he imagine
so vile, and base, as to be a coward towards men, and a boaster towards
God?" (Montaigne, II, xviii, 603). Bacon alludes to the passage in his
essay, "Of Truth": "And therefore Mountaigny saith prettily, when he
inquired the reason, why the word of the lie should be such a disgrace and
such an odious charge? saith he, *If it be well weighed, to say that a man lieth, is
as much to say as that he is brave towards God and a coward towards men.* For a
lie faces God, and shrinks from man."
413. *fondly*] foolishly.

No, we'll be wise; this night our daughter yields
Your father's answer. This night we invite   415
Your presence therefore to a feastful waking.
Tomorrow to Ferrara you return,
With wished answer to your royal father.
Meantime, as you respect our best relation
Of your fair bearing (Granuffo, is't not good?)—   420
Of your fair bearing, rest more anxious
(No, anxious is not a good word)—rest more vigilant
Over your passion, both forbear and bear,
Anechou è apechou (that's Greek to you now)—
Else your youth shall find   425
Our nose not stuff'd, but we can take the wind
And smell you out—I say no more but thus—
And smell you out. What, ha' not we our eyes,
Our nose and ears? What, are these hairs unwise?
Look to't, *quos ego*—(a figure called *aposiopesis* or *increpatio*.) 430
                              Exeunt Gonzago *and* Granuffo.

                    Tiberio *reads the embroidered scarves.*

TIBERIO.
    "Prove you but justly loving and conceive me,
    Justice shall leave the gods before I leave thee."—
    Imagination prove as true as thou art sweet!—
    "And though the duke seem wise, he'll find this strain,
    When two hearts yield consent, all thwarting's vain."—   435
    O, quick, deviceful, strong-brain'd Dulcimel!
    Thou art too full of wit to be a wife.

---

424. *Anechou è apechou*] *Anechon, e*   430. *quos*] *Q1–2; quot 1633.*
apechon Q1; Anexou è ampexou Q2.   430.2.] *Q2; not in Q1.*

---

424. *Anechou è apechou*] "abstain and avoid." The reference is to the
maxim of Epictetus (reported by Aulus Gellius, xvii. 19)—"Ἀνέχου καὶ
Ἀπέχου" (Bullen).
    430. *quos ego*—] "Whom I—" (Virgil, *Aeneid*, I.135). Quoted as an
example of aposiopesis by Quintilian (IX. ii. 54): "*Aposiopesis*, which Cicero
calls *reticentia*, Celsus *obticentia*, and some *interruptio*, is used to indicate
passion or anger, as in the line: 'Whom I—/ But better first these billows
to assuage.'"
    430. *increpatio*] "a chiding or threatning" (Thomas Thomas, *Dictionarium*,
ed. 1596).

Why dost thou love? Or what strong heat gave life
To such faint hopes? O, woman, thou art made
Most only of, and for deceit. Thy form   440
Is nothing but delusion of our eyes,
Our ears, our hearts, and sometimes of our hands;
Hypocrisy and vanity brought forth,
Without male heat, thy most, most monstrous being!
Shall I abuse my royal father's trust,   445
And make myself a scorn, the very food
Of rumor infamous? Shall I, that ever loathed
A thought of woman, now begin to love
My worthy father's right? break faith to him
That got me, to get a faithless woman?   450

HERCULES.

True, my worthy lord, your grace is *verè pius*.

TIBERIO.

To take from my good father the pleasure of his eyes,
And of his hands, imaginary solace of his fading life.

HERCULES.

His life that only lives to your sole good!

TIBERIO.

And my self good, his life's most only end.   455

HERCULES.

Which, O, may never end!

TIBERIO.

Yes, Fawn, in time. We must not prescribe to nature everything. There's some end in everything.

HERCULES.

But in a woman. Yet as she is a wife, she is oftentimes the
end of her husband.   460

TIBERIO.

Shall I, I say?—

HERCULES.

Shall you, I say, confound your own fair hopes,
Cross all your course of life, make yourself vain
To your once steady graveness, and all to second
The ambitious quickness of a monstrous love,   465

---

451. *verè pius*] truly pious.
463. *Cross*] thwart.

That's only out of difficulty born,
And followed only for the miracle
In the obtaining? I would ha' ye now,
Tell her father all.

TIBERIO.   Uncompassionate, vild man,
   Shall I not pity, if I cannot love?   470
   Or rather shall I not for pity love
   So wondrous wit in so most wondrous beauty,
   That with such rarest art and cunning means
   Entreats what I (thing valueless) am not
   Worthy but to grant, my admiration?   475
   Are fathers to be thought on in our loves?

HERCULES.
   True right, sir. Fathers or friends, a crown and love
   Hath none, but are allied to themselves alone.
   Your father, I may boldly say, he's an ass,
   To hope that you'll forbear to swallow   480
   What he cannot chew. Nay 'tis injustice, truly,
   For him to judge it fit that you should starve
   For that which only he can feast his eye withal,
   And not digest.

TIBERIO.
   O, Fawn, what man of so cold earth   485
   But must love such a wit in such a body?
   Thou last and only rareness of heaven's works,
   From best of man made model of the gods!
   Divinest woman, thou perfection
   Of all proportion's beauty, made when Jove was blithe,   490
   Well filled with nectar, and full friends with man.
   Thou dear as air, necessary as sleep
   To careful man! Woman, O, who can sin so deeply
   As to be curs'd from knowing of the pleasures
   Thy soft society, modest amorousness,   495
   Yields to our tedious life! Fawn, the duke shall not know
   this.

---

474. I (thing . . .) am] *Q2;* I   478. but are] *Q2;* but all are *Q1.*
thinke . . . and *Q1.*

---

469. *vild*] vile.

HERCULES.

Unless you tell him. But what hope can live in you
When your short stay, and your most shorten'd conference,
Not only actions, but even looks observ'd,   500
Cut off all possibilities of obtaining?

TIBERIO.

Tush, Fawn, to violence of women's love and wit,
Nothing but not obtaining is impossible.
Notumque furens quid faemina possit.

HERCULES.

But then how rest you to your father true?   505

TIBERIO.

To him that only can give dues, she rests most due.   *Exit.*

HERCULES.

Even so? He that with safety would well lurk in courts
To best elected ends, of force is wrung
To keep broad eyes, soft feet, long ears, and most short
   tongue;
For 'tis of knowing creatures the main art   510
To use quick hams, wide arms, and most close heart.

[IV.i]   *Enter* Hercules *and* Garbetza.

HERCULES.

Why 'tis a most well-in-fashion affection, Donna Garbetza.
Your knight, Sir Amorous, is a man of a most unfortunate
back, spits white, has an ill breath, at three after dinner
goes to the bath, takes the diet, nay, which is more, takes
tobacco; therefore, with great authority, you may cuckold   5
him.

511.1.] *Actus tertii finis. Q 1–2.*   3. breath] *Q2;* breath, and *Q1.*
[IV.i]

---

504. *Notumque . . . possit*] "It is knowne what a woman may/ Whose
raging passions have no stay" (Virgil, *Aeneid*, V. 6; quoted in Montaigne,
III, v, 780).
511. *hams*] thighs, here active ("quick") in making courtly bows.
511. *close*] secret.

GARBETZA.

I hope so, but would that friend my brother discover me,
would he wrong himself to prejudice me?

HERCULES.

No prejudice, dear Garbetza; his brother your husband,
right; he cuckold his eldest brother, true; he gets her with   10
child, just.

GARBETZA.

Sure, there's no wrong in right, true, and just.

HERCULES.

And indeed, since the virtue of procreation growed hopeless
in your husband, to whom should you rather commit your
love and honor to, than him that is most like and near   15
your husband, his brother? But are you assured your friend
and brother rests entirely constant solely to you?

GARBETZA.

To me? O, Fawn, let me sigh it with joy into thy bosom,
my brother has been wooed by this and that and t'other
lady to entertain them (for I ha' seen their letters) but his   20
vow to me, O Fawn, is most immutable, unfeigning,
peculiar, and indeed deserved.

Enter Puttota *and a* Page, Puttota *with a letter in her hand.*
[Hercules *and* Garbetza *conceal themselves.*]

PUTTOTA.

Never entreat me, never beseech me to have pity forsooth
on your master, M. Herod. Let him never be so daringly
ambitious as to hope with all his vows and protestations to   25
gain my affection. Gods my discretion! Has my sutlery,
tapstry, laundry made me be ta'en up at the court? Preferr'd me to a husband? And have I advanc'd my husband,
with the labor of mine own body, from the black guard to

22.1. her] *Bullen;* his *Q 1–2.*

---

7. *brother*] brother-in-law (Herod).
24. M.] "As I am not sure whether we should read 'Master' or 'Messer,'
(*Ital.*), I follow the old copies" (Bullen).
26. *sutlery*] providing provisions.
27. *tapstry*] drawing ale.
29. *black guard*] kitchen drudges.

be one of the duke's drummers, to make him one of the court   30
forkers? Shall I that purify many lords and some ladies,
can tell who wears perfumes, who plasters, and for why,
know who's a gallant of a chaste shirt and who not; shall I
become, or dares your master think I will become, or if I
would become, presumes your master to hope I would   35
become one of his common feminines? No, let M. Herod
brag of his brother's wife. I scorn his letters and her
leavings at my heel, i'faith, and so tell him.

PAGE.

Nay softly, dear Puttota, Mistress Puttota, Madam Puttota,
O, be merciful to my languishing master. He may in time   40
grow a great and well-grac'd courtier, for he wears yellow
already. Mix therefore your loves. As for Madam Garbetza,
his brother's wife, you see what he writes there.

PUTTOTA.

I must confess he says she is a spiny, green creature, of an
unwholesome barren blood and cold embrace, a bony thing   45
of most unequal hips, uneven eyes, ill-rank'd teeth, and
indeed one, but that she hires him, he endures not. Yet, for
all this, does he hope to dishonest me? I am for his betters.
I would he should well know it, for more by many than my
husband know I am a woman of a known, sound, and   50
upright carriage, and so he shall find if he deal with me,
and so tell him, I pray you. What, does he hope to make me
one of his gills, his punks, polecats, flirts, and feminines?

Exit. As Puttota *goes out, she flings away the letter. The* Page *puts it up,
and as he is talking,* Hercules *steals it out of his pocket.*

PAGE.

Alas, my miserable master, what suds art thou wash'd

---

31. forkers] *Q2;* gallants *Q1.*   39. softly] *Dilke, Bullen;* costlie
31. Shall . . . ladies] *Q2; not in Q1.*   *Q1–2, 1633, Wood.*
33. and who . . . shall] *Q2; not in*   41. a] *Q1; not in Q2.*
Q1, 1633.   41. yellow] *Q2;* greene *Q1.*
35. would] *Q2; not in Q1.*

---

30. *drummer*] one who gathers recruits.
31. *forkers*] cuckolds.
41. *yellow*] like green (see textual note), a sign of jealousy.
53. *gills . . . feminines*] cant terms for "prostitute."
54. *suds*] dregs.

into? Thou art born to be scorn'd of every carted com- 55
munity! And yet he'll outcrack a German when he is drunk,
or a Spaniard after he hath eaten a fumatho, that he has lien
with that and that and t'other lady, that he lay last night
in such a madonna's chamber, t'other night he lay in such a
countess's couch, tonight he lies in such a lady's closet, 60
when poor I know all this while he only lied in his throat.

Exit.

HERCULES [*reads*].

"Madam, let me sigh it in your bosom, how immutable
and unfainting and indeed—"

GARBETZA.

Fawn, I will undo that rascal. He shall starve for any
further maintenance.   65

HERCULES.

You may make him come to the covering and recovering of
his old doublets.

GARBETZA.

He was in fair hope of proving heir to his elder brother,
but he has gotten me with child.

HERCULES.

So, you withdrawing your favor, his present means fail him; 70
and by getting you with child, his future means forever rest
despairful to him.

GARBETZA.

O heaven, that I could curse him beneath damnation,
impudent varlet. By my reputation, Fawn, I only lov'd
him because I thought I only did not love him. He vowed 75
infinite beauties doted on him. Alas, I was a simple country
lady, wore gold buttons, trunk sleeves, and flaggon bracelets.
In this state of innocency was I brought up to the court.

HERCULES.

And now instead of country innocency, have you got

59. madonna's] *Q2;* maiden's *Q1.*   64. that] *Q2;* it *Q1.*
59. lay] *Q2;* laide *Q1;* layd *1633.*   69. me with] *Q2;* a *Q1.*
61. only] *Q2; not in Q1.*

---

55. *carted*] punishment for prostitutes.
56. *outcrack*] out brag.
57. *fumatho*] fumade (a smoked pilchard).
77. *trunk sleeves*] "Large sleeves, stuffed with wool, hair, etc." (Bullen).

court honesty. Well, madam, leave your brother to my   80
placing. He shall have a special cabin in the ship of fools.

GARBETZA.

Right. Remember he got his elder brother's wife with
child, and so depriv'd himself of th' inheritance.

HERCULES.

That will stow him under hatches, I warrant you.

GARBETZA.

And so depriv'd himself of inheritance. Dear Fawn, be my   85
champion.

HERCULES.

The very scourge of your most basely offending brother.

GARBETZA.

Ignoble villain, that I might but see thee wretched without
pity and recovery. Well—   [*Exit.*]

Enter Herod *and* Nymphadoro.

HERCULES.

Stand, Herod. You are full met, sir.   90

HEROD.

But not met full, sir. I am as gaunt as a hunting gelding
after three train'd scents. 'Fore Venus, Fawn, I have been
shaling of peascods. Upon four great madonnas have I this
afternoon grafted the forked tree.

HERCULES.

Is't possible?   95

HEROD.

Possible? Fie on this satiety, 'tis a dull, blunt, weary, and
drowsy passion. Who would be a proper fellow to be thus
greedily devoured and swallowed among ladies? Faith,
'tis my torment, my very rack.

84. stow] *Q2;* follow *Q1 1633.*   fanne *Q2;* Fan *1633.*
92. Fawn] *Bullen;* Fanne *Q1;*   93. four great] *Q2;* faire *Q1.*

93. *shaling*] freeing from the shell or husk.
94. *grafted ... tree*] coupled with. "He would hardly have persuaded
Calisthenes to refuse his faire daughter Agarista to Hippoclides because he
had seene him graft the forked tree in her upon a table." (Montaigne,
II, xii, 527).

HERCULES.

Right, Herod, true, for imagine all a man possess'd with a 100
perpetual pleasure, like that of generation, even in the
highest lusciousness, he straight sinks as unable to bear so
continual, so pure, so universal a sensuality.

HEROD.

By even truth, 'tis very right, and for my part would I were
eunuch'd rather than thus suck'd away with kisses, en- 105
feebling dalliance, and—O, the falling sickness on them all!
Why did reasonable nature give so strange, so rebellious,
so tyrannous, so insatiate parts of appetite to so weak a
governess as woman?

HERCULES.

Or why, O custom, didst thou oblige them to modesty, such 110
cold temperance, that they must be wooed by men, courted
by men? Why, all know they are more full of strong
desires, those desires most impatient of delay or hindrance;
they have more unruly passions than men, and weaker
reason to temper those passions than men.   115

NYMPHADORO.

Why then hath not the discretion of nature thought it just
that customary coyness, old fashions, terms of honor and of
modesty forsooth, all laid aside, they court not us, beseech
not us, rather, for sweets of love, than we them? Why? By
Janus, women are but men turn'd the wrong side outward. 120

HERCULES.

O, sir, nature is a wise workman. She knows right well
that if women should woo us to the act of love, we should all
be utterly sham'd. How often should they take us un-
provided, when they are always ready?

HEROD.

Ay, sir, right, sir. To some few such unfortunate hand- 125
some fellows as myself am, to my grief I know it.

HERCULES.

Why, here are two perfect creatures. The one, Nymphadoro,
loves all, and my Herod here enjoys all.

---

100. with] *Q1 corr., Q2;* were *Q1*   114. unruly] *Q2;* unourely *Q1;*
uncorr., 1633.   unhourely *1633.*
109. as] *Q1, 1633;* a *Q2.*   117. that] *Q2; not in Q1.*

HEROD.

Faith, some score or two of ladies or so ravish me among
them, divide my presence, and would indeed engross me 130
were I indeed such an ass as to be made a monopoly of.
Look, sirrah, what a vild hand one of them writes. Who
would ever take this for a "d," "dearest," or read this for
"only," "only dearest."

HERCULES.

Here's a "lie" indeed. 135

HEROD.

True, but here's another much more legible, a good
secretary: "My most affected Herod, the utmost ambition
of my hopes and only—"

HERCULES.

There is one "lie" better shap'd by odds.

HEROD.

Right, but here's a lady's roman hand to me is beyond all. 140
Look ye: "To her most elected servant and worthy friend,
Herod Baldonzozo, Esquire." I believe thou knowest what
countess's hand this is. I'll show thee another.

HERCULES.

No, good Herod, I'll show thee one now: "To his most
elected mistress and worthy laundress, divine mistress 145
Puttota at her tent in the woodyard, or elsewhere, give
these—"

HEROD.

Prithee ha' silence, what's that!

---

130. presence] *Q1;* presents *Q2.*

130. *engross*] monopolize.
135. *"lie"*] Here, and at l. 139, a quibble on (1) the meaning "falsehood"
and (2) on the second syllable of "only" (ll. 134 and 138), often spelled
"onlie" in the early seventeenth century.
137. *secretary*] a style of handwriting used chiefly in legal documents,
imitated in black-letter type.
139. *by odds*] by several times.
140. *roman*] a round and bold handwriting, similar to ancient Roman
inscriptions.
142. *Baldonzozo*] cf. I.ii.301.n.

HERCULES.

"If my tears or vows, my faithful'st protestations on my
knees—"   150

HEROD.

Good, hold.

HERCULES.

"Fair and only loved laundress—"

HEROD.

Forbear, I beseech thee.

HERCULES.

"Might move thy stony heart to take pity on my sighs—"

HEROD.

Do not shame me to the day of judgment.   155

HERCULES.

"Alas, I write it in passion. Alas, thou knowest besides
my loathed sister, thou art—"

HEROD.

For the Lord's sake.

HERCULES.

"The only hope of my pleasure, the only pleasure of my
hopes. Be pleas'd therefore to—"   160

HEROD.

Cease, I beseech thee.

HERCULES.

Pish, ne'er blush man, 'tis an uncourtly quality. As for thy
lying, as long as there's policy in't, it is very passable.
Wherefore has heaven given man tongue but to speak to a
man's own glory? He that cannot swell bigger than his   165
natural skin, nor seem to be in more grace than he is,
has not learn'd the very rudiments or A, B, C, of courtship.

HEROD.

Upon my heart, Fawn, thou pleasest me to the soul. Why,
look you, for mine own part, I must confess—

Enter Dondolo.

See, here's the duke's fool.   170

DONDOLO.

Aboard, aboard, aboard! All manner of fools of court,

149. faithful'st] *Q2;* doubtlest *Q1.*

-75-

city, or country, of what degree, sex, or nature.
HEROD.
    Fool?
DONDOLO.
    Herod?
HERCULES.
    What, are ye full freighted? Is your ship well fool'd?   175
DONDOLO.
    O, 'twas excellently thronged full. A justice of peace,
though he had been one of the most illiterate asses in a
country, could hardly ha' got a hanging cabin. O, we had
first some long fortunate great politicians, that were so
sottishly paradised as to think, when popular hate seconded 180
princes' displeasure to them, any unmerited violence could
seem to the world injustice; some purple fellows whom
chance reared, and their own deficiencies of spirit hurled
down. We had some courtiers that o'erbought their offices,
and yet durst fall in love; priests that forsook their functions 185
to avoid a thwart stroke with a wet finger. But now, alas,
Fawn, now there's space and place.
HERCULES.
    Why, how gat all these forth? Was not the warrant strong?
DONDOLO.
    Yes, yes, but they got a supersedeas. All of them proved
themselves either knaves or madmen and so were all let go. 190
There's none left now in our ship but a few citizens that
let their wives keep their shopbooks, some philosophers,
and a few critics; one of which critics has lost his flesh with
fishing at the measure of Plautus' verses; another has vow'd
to get the consumption of the lungs, or to leave to posterity 195

187. space . . . place] *Q2;* place
. . . place *Q1.*

---

178. *hanging cabin*] since "cabin" meant "berth," a hanging cabin
might be a hammock, the poorest accommodation.
182. *purple fellows*] gaudy courtiers.
186. *thwart . . . finger*] being rubbed off the preferred list; "with a wet
finger" means "easily."
189. *supersedeas*] writ staying legal action (*OED*).
194–196. *measure . . . verses . . . orthography*] "He will either die in his
pursuit, or teach posteritie the measure of *Plautus* verses, and the true Orthography of a Latine word." (Montaigne, I, xxxviii, 192).

the true orthography and pronunciation of laughing; a
third hath melted a great deal o' suet, worn out his thumbs
with turning, read out his eyes, and studied his face out of a
sanguine into a meager, spawling, fleamy loathsomeness,
and all to find but why *mentula* should be the feminine 200
gender, since the rule is *Propria qua maribus tribuuntur mascula
dicas.* These philosophers, critics, and all the maids we could
find at sixteen, are all our freight now.

HERCULES.

O, then, your ship of fools is full?

NYMPHADORO.

True, the maids at seventeen fill it.   205

DONDOLO.

Fill it, quoth you. Alas, we have very few, and these we
were fain to take up in the country, too.

HERCULES.

But what philosophers ha' ye?

DONDOLO.

O, very strange fellows. One knows nothing; dares not
aver he lives, goes, sees, feels.   210

NYMPHADORO.

A most insensible philosopher.

DONDOLO.

Another, that there is no present time, and that one man
today and tomorrow is not the same man; so that he that
yesterday owed money, today owes none, because he is not
the same man.   215

198–199. *read . . . spawling*] "This man . . . thou seest come out of his
study meagre-looking, with eyes-trilling, flegmatike, squalide, and spauling,
doest thou thinke, that plodding on his books he doth seek how he shall
become an honester man; or more wise, or more content?" (Montaigne,
I, xxxviii, 192). *Spawling* means "spitting copiously."

200. *mentula*] penis.

201–202. *Propria . . . dicas*] Things attributed to males should be called
masculine.

212–215. *no present time . . . same man*] "The Stoics affirm, there is no
present time, and that which we call present, is but conjoyning and
assembling of future time and past. . . . Epicarmus avoucheth that who
ere while borrowed any mony, doth not now owe it; . . . since they are no
more themselves, but are become others. . . ." (Montaigne, II, xii, 545).

HEROD.

Would that philosophy would hold good in law!

HERCULES.

But why has the duke thus labor'd to have all the fools
shipp'd out of his dominions?

DONDOLO.

Marry, because he would play the fool himself alone, without any rival.   220

HERCULES.

'Ware your breech, fool.

DONDOLO.

I warrant thee, old lad, 'tis the privilege of poor fools to
talk before an intelligencer. Marry, if I could fool myself
into a lordship, as I know some ha' fool'd themselves out
of a lordship—were I grown some huge fellow and got the 225
leer of the people upon me, if the fates had so decreed it—
I should talk treason, though I ne'er open'd my lips.

HERCULES.

Indeed, *fatis agimur, cedite fatis!* But how runs rumor?
What breath's strongest in the palace now? I think you
know all.   230

DONDOLO.

Yes, we fools think we know all. The prince hath audience
tonight, is feasted, and after supper is entertain'd with no
comedy, masque, or barriers, but with—

NYMPHADORO.

What, I prithee?

HEROD.

What, I prithee?   .   235

DONDOLO.

With a most new and special shape of delight.

NYMPHADORO.

What, for Jove's sake?

216. philosophy] *1633;* Philos-   224. fool'd] *1633;* foole *Q1-2.*
opher *Q1-2.*   228. Indeed] *Q2;* In *Q1, 1633.*

---

221. *'Ware . . . fool*] fools could be whipped for too free speech.
223. *intelligencer*] cf. I.ii.203.
228. *fatis . . . fatis*] We are driven by fate, give in to it!
229. *breath*] voice.
233. *barriers*] staged combat, fought on foot with swords.

DONDOLO.

Marry, gallants, a session, a general council of love
summon'd in the name of Don Cupid, to which upon pain of
their mistress' displeasure shall appear all favor-wearers, 240
sonnet-mongers, health-drinkers, and neat enrichers of
barbers and perfumers. And to conclude, all that can
wyhee or wag the tail are, upon grievous pains of their back,
summon'd to be assistant in that session of love.

HERCULES.

Hold, hold! Do not pall the delight before it come to our 245
palate. And what other rumor keeps air in men's lungs?

DONDOLO.

O, the egregiousness of folly! Ha' you not heard of Don
Zuccone?

NYMPHADORO.

What of him, good fool?

DONDOLO.

He is separated.   250

NYMPHADORO.

Divorc'd?

DONDOLO.

That salt, that criticism, that very all epigram of a woman,
that analysis, that compendium of wittiness—

NYMPHADORO.

Now, Jesu, what words the fool has!

DONDOLO.

We ha' still such words, but I will not unshale the jest 255
before it be ripe, and therefore kissing your worship's
fingers in most sweet terms without any sense, and with
most fair looks without any good meaning, I most courtlike
take my leave, *basilus manus de vostro signioria.*

HEROD.

Stay, fool, we'll follow thee; for, 'fore heaven, we must 260
prepare ourselves for this session.   *Exeunt [all but* Hercules].

241. enrichers] *Q2;* in riches *Q1,*
1633.
246. in] *Q2;* on *Q1, 1633.*
247. O, the] *Q2;* Other *Q1, 1633.*

253. wittiness] *Q2;* witnes *Q1,*
1633.
255. unshale] *Q2;* unshake *Q1,*
1633.

255. *unshale*] cf. IV.i.93.n.
259. *basilus manus*] kiss the hands; "corrupt Spanish for *besar los manos*"
(Bullen).

Enter Zuccone, *pursued by* Zoya *on her knees, attended by Ladies.*

ZUCCONE.

    I will have no mercy, I will not relent. Justice' beard is
shaven, and it shall give thee no hold. I am separated, and
I will be separated.

ZOYA.

    Dear my lord, husband.   265

ZUCCONE.

    Hence, creature! I am none of thy husband, or father of
thy bastard. No, I will be tyrannous, and a most deep
revenger. The order shall stand. Ha, thou quean, I ha' no
wife now.

ZOYA.

    Sweet, my lord.   270

ZUCCONE.

    Hence! avaunt! I will marry a woman with no womb, a
creature with two noses, a wench with no hair, rather
than remarry thee. Nay, I will first marry—mark me—
I will first marry—observe me—I will rather marry a
woman that with thirst drinks the blood of man. Nay— 275
heed me—a woman that will thrust in crowds, a lady that,
being with child, ventures the hope of her womb, nay,
gives two crowns for a room to behold a goodly man three
parts alive quartered, his privities hackled off, his belly
launch'd up. Nay, I'll rather marry a woman to whom 280
these smoking, hideous, bloodful, horrid, though most
just spectacles, are very lust, rather than re-accept thee.
Was I not a handsome fellow, from my foot to my feather?
Had I not wit? Nay, which is more, was I not a Don,
and didst thou Actaeon me? Did I not make thee a lady? 285

---

281. these] *1633;* this *Q1–2.*

    277. *ventures*] hazards.
    278. *crown*] five shillings.
    279. *quartered*] cut into quarters; the punishment for treason.
    280. *launch'd*] lanced, gashed.
    282. *lust*] delight.
    285. *Actaeon me*] make a cuckold of me (with reference to the horns of the
stag into which Actaeon was metamorphosed).

HERCULES.

And did she not make you a more worshipful thing, a
cuckold?

ZUCCONE.

I married thee in hope of children.

HERCULES.

And has not she showed herself fruitful that was got with
child without help of her husband?   290

ZUCCONE.

Ha, thou ungrateful, immodest, unwise, and one that,
God's my witness, I ha' lov'd. But go thy ways, twist with
whom thou wilt. For my part, th'ast spun a fair thread.
Who'll kiss thee now? Who'll court thee now? Who'll ha'
thee now?   295

ZOYA.

Pity the frailty of my sex, sweet lord.

ZUCCONE.

No, pity is a fool, and I will not wear his coxcomb. I
have vow'd to loathe thee. The Irishman shall hate *aqua
vitae*, the Welshman cheese, the Dutchman shall loathe
salt butter, before I relove thee. Does the babe pule? Thou 300
shouldst ha' cried before, 'tis too late now. No, the trees
in autumn shall sooner call back the spring with shedding of
their leaves, than thou reverse my just, irrevocable hatred
with thy tears. Away! go! vaunt!   *Exeunt* Zoya *and the ladies.*

HERCULES.

Nay, but most of this is your fault, that for many years, 305
only upon mere mistrust, sever'd your body from your lady,
and in that time gave opportunity, turn'd a jealous ass, and
hired some to try and tempt your lady's honor, whilst she,
with all possible industry of apparent merit, diverting your
unfortunate suspicion—   310

291. one] *Q2; not in Q1.*   307–308. and hired some to] *Q1*
297. his] *Q1;* hir *Q2.*   *corr.;* and heard some so *Q1 uncorr.,*
304. *Exeunt . . . ladies*] *Bullen; Exit*   *1633;* hired and some to *Q2.*
. . . *lady Q1–2.*

292. *twist*] join.
298–300. *Irishman . . . butter*] cf. *Merry Wives of Windsor,* II.ii.317–320
(Wood).

ZUCCONE.

I know't, I confess. All this I did, and I do glory in't.
Why, cannot a young lady for many months keep honest?
No, I misthought it. My wife had wit, beauty, health,
good birth, fair clothes, and a passing body; a lady of rare
discourse, quick eye, sweet language, alluring behavior, 315
and exquisite entertainment. I misthought it, I fear'd,
I doubted, and at the last I found it out, I praise my wit.
I knew I was a cuckold.

HERCULES.

An excellent wit.

ZUCCONE.

True, Fawn; you shall read of few dons that have had such 320
a wit, I can tell you; and I found it out that I was a
cuckold.

HERCULES.

Which now you have found, you will not be such an ass as
Caesar, great Pompey, Lucullus, Anthony, or Cato, and
divers other Romans, cuckolds, who all knew it, and yet 325
were ne'er divorc'd upon't; or like that smith-god Vulcan,
who, having taken his wife taking, yet was presently
appeased, and entreated to make an armor for a bastard of
hers, Aeneas.

ZUCCONE.

No, the Romans were asses, and thought that a woman 330
might mix her thigh with a stranger wantonly, and yet still
love her husband matrimonially.

HERCULES.

As indeed they say many married men lie sometime with
strange women, whom, but for the instant use, they abhor.

ZUCCONE.

And as for Vulcan, 'twas humanity more than human. Such 335

---

320. few dons] *Q2 corr., Wood;*   321. that] *Q2; & Q1.*
some Lords *Q2 uncorr., Bullen;* few   327. taking] *Q2; not in Q1.*
dunces *Q1, 1633.*   329. Aeneas] *Q2; not in Q1.*

324–326. *Caesar ... divorc'd*] "Lucullus, Caesar, Pompey, Anthony,
Cato, and divers other gallant men were Cuckolds, and knew it, though
they made no stirre about it" (Montaigne, III, v, 778).

excess of goodness, for my part, only belong to the gods.

HERCULES.

Ass for you—

ZUCCONE.

As for me, my Fawn, I am a bachelor now.

HERCULES.

But you are a cuckold still, and one that knows himself to
be a cuckold.   340

ZUCCONE.

Right, that's it. And I knew it not, 'twere nothing. And
if I had not pursu'd it too, it had lien in oblivion, and
shadowed in doubt, but now I ha' blaz'd it.

HERCULES.

The world shall know what you are.

ZUCCONE.

True, I'll pocket up no horns, but my revenge shall speak in 345
thunder.

HERCULES.

Indeed, I must confess I know twenty are cuckolds, honestly
and decently enough. A worthy gallant spirit (whose virtue
suppresseth his mishap) is lamented but not disesteem'd
by it. Yet the world shall know—   350

ZUCCONE.

I am none of those silent coxcombs. It shall out.

HERCULES.

And although it be no great part of injustice for him to be
struck with the scabbard that has struck with the blade (for
there is few of us but hath made someone cuckold or
other)—   355

ZUCCONE.

True, I ha' done't myself.

HERCULES.

Yet—

336. only] *Q2;* shal onely *Q1.*   *Q2;* and decently and stately *Q1.*
347–348. honestly and decently]   351. out] *Q2;* not *Q1.*

_____

345. *pocket up*] conceal.
351. *coxcombs*] fools.

ZUCCONE.

Yet I hope a man of wit may prevent his own mishap, or
if he cannot prevent it—

HERCULES.

Yet—   360

ZUCCONE.

Yet make it known yet, and so known that the world may
tremble with only thinking of it. Well, Fawn, whom
shall I marry now? O heaven, that God made for a man no
other means of procreation and maintaining the world
peopled but by women! O, that we could increase like roses 365
by being slipp'd one from another, or like flies procreate
with blowing, or any other way than by a woman—by
women, who have no reason in their love, or mercy in their
hate, no rule in their pity, no pity in their revenge, no
judgment to speak, and yet no patience to hold their 370
tongues:
Man's opposite, the more held down, they swell;
Above them naught but will, beneath them naught but hell.

HERCULES.

Or, that since heaven hath given us no other means to allay
our furious appetite, no other way of increasing our progeny, 375
since we must entreat and beg for assuagement of our
passions, and entertainment of our affections, why did not
heaven make us a nobler creature than women to sue unto?
Some admirable deity, of an uncorruptible beauty, that
might be worth our knees, the expense of our heat, and 380
the crinkling of our hams.

ZUCCONE.

But that we must court, sonnet, flatter, bribe, kneel, sue
to so feeble and imperfect, inconstant, idle, vain, hollow
bubble, as woman is! O, my Fawn!

359. cannot] *1633;* can   *Q1–2,*   378. sue] *1633;* shew *Q1 corr., Q2;*
Bullen; can't *Wood.*   sa ye *Q1 uncorr.*
365–366. increase . . . another] *Q2;* 380. might] *Q2, 1633; not in Q1.*
get one an other with child Fawn   381. hams] *Q2; — 1633; not in Q1.*
Q1.   384. Fawn] *Q2;* face *Q1.*

373. *will*] "carnal desire or appetite" (*OED*).
381. *crinkling*] twisting.
382. *sonnet*] write a poem in praise of.

HERCULES.

O, my lord, look who here comes.   385

Enter Zoya, *supported by a gentleman usher, followed by* Herod *and*
Nymphadoro *with much state, soft music playing.*

ZUCCONE.

Death o' man, is she delivered?

HERCULES.

Deliver'd? Yes, O my Don, delivered! Yes, Donna Zoya,
the grace of society, the music of sweetly agreeing perfection,
more clearly chaste than ice or frozen rain, that glory of her
sex, that wonder of wit, that beauty more fresh'd than 390
any cool and trembling wind, that now only wish of a man,
is delivered, is delivered!

ZUCCONE.

How?

HERCULES.

From Don Zuccone, that dry scaliness, that sarpego, that
barren drought, and shame of all humanity.   395

ZOYA.

What fellow's that?

NYMPHADORO.

Don Zuccone, your sometime husband.

Enter Philocalia.

ZOYA.

Alas, poor creature.

PHILOCALIA.

The princess prays your company.

ZOYA.

I wait upon her pleasure.   400

All but Hercules, Zuccone, Herod, *and* Nymphadoro *depart.*

ZUCCONE.

Gentleman, why hazard you your reputation in shameful
company with such a branded creature?

390. fresh'd] *Q2;* freshy *Q1;*
freshly *1633.*

---

394. *sarpego*] serpigo, a ringworm-like disease.

HEROD.

Miserable man, whose fortune were beyond tears to be
pitied, but that thou art the ridiculous author of thine own
laugh'd-at mischief. 405

ZUCCONE.

Without paraphrase, your meaning?

NYMPHADORO.

Why, thou woman's fool—

ZUCCONE.

Good gentlemen, let one die but once.

HEROD.

Was not thou most curstfully mad to sever thyself from
such an unequal'd rarity? 410

ZUCCONE.

Is she not a strumpet? Is she not with child?

NYMPHADORO.

Yes, with feathers.

HERCULES.

Why, weakness of reason, couldst not perceive all was
feign'd to be rid of thee?

ZUCCONE.

Of me? 415

NYMPHADORO.

She with child? Untrodden snow is not so spotless.

HEROD.

Chaste as the first voice of a newborn infant.

HERCULES.

Know, she grew loathing of thy jealousy.

NYMPHADORO.

Thy most pernicious curiosity.

HERCULES.

Whose suspicions made her unimitable graces motive of thy 420
base jealousy.

HEROD.

Why, beast of man!

NYMPHADORO.

Wretched above expression, that snored'st over a beauty
which thousands desired, neglectedst her bed, for whose

424. neglectedst] *1633;* neglecst
Q *1–2.*

enjoying a very saint would have sued.   425

HERCULES.

Defam'd her!

HEROD.

Suggested privily against her!

NYMPHADORO.

Gave foul language publicly of her!

HERCULES.

And now, lastly, done that for her which she only pray'd
for, and wish'd as wholesome air for, namely, to be rid 430
from such an unworthy—

HEROD.

Senseless—

NYMPHADORO.

Injurious—

HERCULES.

Malicious—

HEROD.

Suspicious—   435

NYMPHADORO.

Misshaped—

HERCULES.

Ill-languag'd—

HEROD.

Unworthy—

NYMPHADORO.

Ridiculous—

HERCULES.

Jealous—   440

HEROD.

Arch coxcomb as thou art!   *Exeunt* Nymphadoro *and* Herod.

ZUCCONE.

O, I am sick, my blood has the cramp, my stomach o'erturns.

O, I am very sick.

HERCULES.

Why, my sweet Don, you are no cuckold.

ZUCCONE.

That's the grief on't.   445

---

430. rid] *Q2; not in Q1.*

445–447. That's . . . That] *Q2; Zuc.*

That's the griefe on't *Herc.* that's
the griefe ont that *Q1.*

HERCULES.

That's—

ZUCCONE.

That I ha' wrong'd so sweet (and now, in my knowledge) so delicate a creature! O methinks I embrace her yet.

HERCULES.

Alas, my lord, you have done her no wrong, no wrong in the world. You have done her a pleasure, a great pleasure. A   450
thousand gentlemen, nay dukes, will be proud to accept your leavings—your leavings! Now is she courted! This heir sends her jewels, that lord proffers her jointures, t'other knight proclaims challenges to maintain her the only not beautiful but very beauty of women.   455

ZUCCONE.

But I shall never embrace her more.

HERCULES.

Nay, that's true, that's most true. I would not afflict you, only think how unrelentless you were to her but supposed fault.

ZUCCONE.

O, 'tis true, too true.   460

HERCULES.

Think how you scorn'd her tears.

ZUCCONE.

Most right.

HERCULES.

Tears that were only shed—I would not vex you—in very grief to see you covet your own shame.

ZUCCONE.

Too true, too true.   465

HERCULES.

For, indeed, she is the sweetest modest soul, the fullest of pity.

ZUCCONE.

O yes, O yes.

468. O yes, O yes] *Q2;* O I O I Q *1.*

_____

453. *jointures*] property held "to the joint use of husband and wife for life or in tail, as a provision for the latter during widowhood" (*OED*).

HERCULES.

The softness and very courtesy of her sex, as one that
never lov'd any—   470

ZUCCONE.

But me.

HERCULES.

So much that he might hope to dishonor her, nor any so
little that he might fear she disdain'd him. O, the graces
made her a soul as soft as spotless down upon the swan's
fair breast that drew bright Cytherea's chariot. Yet think 475
(I would not vex you), yet think how cruel you were to her.

ZUCCONE.

As a tiger, as a very tiger.

HERCULES.

And never hope to be reconcil'd, never dream to be reconcil'd, never.

ZUCCONE.

Never? Alas, good Fawn, what wouldst wish me to do now? 480

HERCULES.

Faith, go hang yourself, my Don. That's best, sure.

ZUCCONE.

Nay, that's too good, for I'll do worse than that, I'll marry
again. Where canst pick out a morsel for me, Fawn?

HERCULES.

There is a modest, matron-like creature—

ZUCCONE.

What years, Fawn?   485

HERCULES.

Some fourscore, wanting one.

ZUCCONE.

A good sober age. Is she wealthy?

HERCULES.

Very wealthy.

ZUCCONE.

Excellent!

HERCULES.

She has three hairs on her scalp and four teeth in her head, 490

473. disdain'd] *Q2;* disclaim'd *Q1.*   *uncorr., 1633.*
476. cruel] *Q2, Q1 corr.,* ciuill *Q1*

a brow wrinkled and pucker'd like old parchment half
burnt. She has had eyes. No woman's jawbones are more
apparent. Her sometimes envious lips now shrink in, and
give her nose and her chin leave to kiss each other very
moistly. As for her reverend mouth, it seldom opens, but the 495
very breath that flies out of it infects the fowls of the air,
and makes them drop down dead. Her breasts hang like
cobwebs. Her flesh will never make you cuckold. Her
bones may.

ZUCCONE.

But is she wealthy?   500

HERCULES.

Very wealthy.

ZUCCONE.

And will she ha' me, art sure?

HERCULES.

No, sure she will not have you. Why, do you think that
a waiting-woman of three bastards, a strumpet nine times
carted, or a hag whose eyes shoot poison, that has been an 505
old witch, and is now turning into a gib-cat, will ha' you?
Marry Don Zuccone, the contempt of women and the shame
of men, that has afflicted, contemn'd so choice a perfection
as Donna Zoya's!

ZUCCONE.

Alas, Fawn, I confess. What wouldst ha' me do?   510

HERCULES.

Hang yourself you shall not, marry you cannot. I'll tell ye
what you shall do. There is a ship of fools setting forth. If
you make good means and entreat hard, you may obtain a
passage, man. Be master's mate, I warrant you.

ZUCCONE.

Fawn, thou art a scurvy bitter knave, and dost flout Dons 515
to their faces. 'Twas thou flattered'st me to this, and now
thou laugh'st at me, dost? Though indeed I had a
certain proclivity, but thou madest me resolute. Dost grin

506. cat] *Q2*; cat, th at *Q1 corr.*;   513. make] *Q2*; see *Q1*; seek *1633*
cat what *Q1 uncorr.*, *1633*.

506. *gib-cat*] spayed cat, or tom cat.

and gern? O you comforters of life, helps in sickness, joys
in death, and preservers of us in our children after death, 520
women, have mercy on me!

HERCULES.

O my Don, that God made no other means of procreation
but by these women! I speak it not to vex you.

ZUCCONE.

O Fawn, thou hast no mercy in thee. Dost thou leer on me?
Well, I'll creep upon my knees to my wife. Dost laugh at 525
me? Dost gern at me? Dost smile? Dost leer on me, dost
thou? O, I am an ass, true, I am a coxcomb. Well, I am mad,
good. A mischief on your cogging tongue, your soothing
throat, your oily jaws, your supple hams, your dissembling
smiles, and O the grand devil on you all! When mischief 530
favors our fortunes, and we are miserably, though justly
wretched,
More pity, comfort, and more help we have
In foes profess'd, than in a flattering knave.   *Exit.*

HERCULES.

Thus few strike sail until they run on shelf;   535
The eye sees all things but his proper self.
In all things curiosity hath been
Vicious at least, but herein most pernicious.
What madness is't to search and find a wound
For which there is no cure, and which unfound   540
Ne'er rankles, whose finding only wounds?
But he that upon vain surmise forsakes
His bed thus long, only to search his shame,
Gives to his wife youth, opportunity,
Keeps her in idleful deliciousness,   545

---

529. hams] *Q2;* thumbes *Q1.*   531. miserably] *Q2;* miserable *Q1.*

---

519. *gern*] "To show the teeth in rage, pain, or disappointment" (*OED*).
528. *cogging*] deceiving.
529. *oily*] slippery, fawning.
535. *shelf*] underwater projection of land.
537–541. *curiosity . . . wounds*] "Curiosity is every where vicious; but
herein pernicious. It is neere folly for one to seeke to be resolved of a doubt,
or search into a mischiefe; for which there is no remedie, but makes it
worse, but festereth the same. . . ." (Montaigne, III, v, 783).

Heats and inflames imagination,
Provokes her to revenge with churlish wrongs—
What should he hope but this? Why should it lie in women,
Or even in chastity itself (since chastity's a female),
T' avoid desires so ripened, such sweets so candied?   550
But she that hath out-borne such mass of wrongs,
Out-dur'd all persecutions, all contempts,
Suspects, disgrace, all wants, and all the mischief,
The baseness of a canker'd churl could cast upon her,
With constant virtue, best feign'd chastity,   555
And in the end turns all his jealousies
To his own scorn, that lady, I implore,
It may be lawful not to praise, but even adore.

Enter Gonzago, Granuffo, *with full state. Enter the cornets sounding.*

GONZAGO.
Are our sports ready? Is the prince at hand?
HERCULES.
The prince is now arriv'd at the court gate.   560
GONZAGO.
What means our daughter's breathless haste?

Enter Dulcimel *in haste.*

DULCIMEL.
O, my princely father, now or never let your princely
wisdom appear.
GONZAGO.
Fear not, our daughter. If it rest within human reason,
I warrant thee. No, I warrant thee, Granuffo, if it rest in   565
man's capacity. Speak, dear daughter.
DULCIMEL.
My lord, the prince—
GONZAGO.
The prince, what of him, dear daughter?
DULCIMEL.
O Lord, what wisdom our good parents need to shield their

551. out-borne] *Q2, 1633;* not
borne *Q1.*

---

555. *feign'd*] fashioned (no pejorative connotation).

chickens from deceits and wiles of kite-like youth.   570

GONZAGO.

Her very phrase displays whose child she is.

DULCIMEL.

Alas, had not your grace been provident,
A very Nestor in advice and knowledge,
Ha! where had you, poor Dulcimel, been now?
What vainness had not I been drawn into!   575

GONZAGO.

'Fore God, she speaks very passionately. Alas, daughter,
heaven gives every man his talent; indeed, virtue and
wisdom are not fortune's gifts; therefore, those that fortune cannot make virtuous, she commonly makes rich.
For our own part, we acknowledge heaven's goodness, 580
and if it were possible to be as wise again as we are, we
would ne'er impute it to ourselves. For as we be flesh and
blood, alas we are fools; but as we are princes, scholars, and
have read *Cicero de Oratore*, I must confess there is another
matter in't. What of the prince, dear daughter?   585

DULCIMEL.

Father, do you see that tree that leans just on my chamber
window?

GONZAGO.

What of that tree?

Enter Tiberio *with his train.*

DULCIMEL.

O, sir, but note the policy of youth;
Mark but the stratagems of working love.   590
The prince salutes me, and thus greets my ear.

GONZAGO.

Speak softly; he is enter'd.

DULCIMEL.

Although he knew I yet stood wavering what to elect
because, though I affected, yet destitute of means to enjoy

575. vainness] *Bullen;* vaines *Q 1–2.*

---

570. *kite-like*] hawk-like.
578–579. *fortune . . . rich*] ". . . fortune . . . having not beene able to make
silly men wise, she hath made them fortunate" (Montaigne, III, viii, 843).

each other, impossibility of having might kill our hope and 595
with our hope desires to enjoy; therefore, to avoid all faint
excuses and vain fears, thus he devised:
To Dulcimel's chamber window
A well-grown plane tree spreads his happy arms.
By that, in depth of night, one may ascend   600
(Despite all father's jealousies and fears)
Into her bed.

GONZAGO.

Speak low; the prince both marks and listens.

DULCIMEL.

You shall provide a priest (quoth he). In truth I promis'd,
and so you well may tell him, for I temporized and only 605
held him off—

GONZAGO.

Politicly; our daughter to a hair.

DULCIMEL.

With full intention to disclose it all to your preventing
wisdom.

GONZAGO.

Ay, let me alone for that. But when intends he this invasion? 610
When will this squirrel climb?

DULCIMEL.

O, sir, in that is all. When but this night?

GONZAGO.

This night?

DULCIMEL.

This very night, when the court revels had o'erwak'd
your spirits, and made them full of sleep, then—   615

GONZAGO.

Then *verbum sat sapienti*! Go, take your chamber, down
upon your knees. Thank God your father is no foolish sot,
but one that can foresee and see.   *Exit* Dulcimel.
My lord, we discharge your presence from our court.

TIBERIO.

What means the duke?   620

596. with] *Q2;* which *Q1.*   599. plane tree] *Q2;* plantaine *Q1.*

616. *verbum . . . sapienti*] a word to the wise is sufficient.

GONZAGO.

> And if tomorrow past you rest in Urbin,
> The privilege of an ambassador
> Is taken from you.

TIBERIO.   Good, your grace, some reason?

GONZAGO.

> What, twice admonish'd, twice again offending,
> And now grown blushless? You promis'd to get into   625
> Her chamber, she to get a priest;
> Indeed she wish'd me tell you she confess'd it;
> And there, despite all father's jealous fears,
> To consummate full joys. Know, sir, our daughter
> Is our daughter, and has wit at will   630
> To gull a thousand easy things like you.
> But, sir, depart; the parliament prepar'd,
> Shall on without you. All the court this night
> Shall triumph that our daughter has escap'd
> Her honor's blowing up. Your end you see.   635
> We speak but short but full, Socratice.

Exit. Remaineth Hercules *and* Tiberio.

TIBERIO.

> What should I think, what hope, what but imagine
> Of these enigmas?

HERCULES.   Sure, sir, the lady loves you
> With violent passion, and this night prepares
> A priest with nuptial rites to entertain you   640
> In her most private chamber.

TIBERIO.   This I know,
> With too much torture, since means are all unknown
> To come unto these ends. Where's this her chamber?
> Then what means shall without suspicion
> Convey me to her chamber? O these doubts   645
> End in despair—

Enter Gonzago *hastily.*

GONZAGO.

> Sir, sir, this plane tree was not planted here

635. honor's] *Q2; not in Q1.*   647. plane tree] *Q2;* Plantine *Q1.*
638. enigmas] *Q2;* engines *Q1.*

---

636. *Socratice*] Socrates was not known for his brevity.

To get into my daughter's chamber, and so she pray'd me
  tell you.
What though the main arms spread into her window,
And easy labor climbs it? Sir, know   650
She has a voice to speak, and bid you welcome
With so full breast that both your ears shall hear on't,
And so she pray'd me tell you. Ha' we no brain?
Youth thinks that age, age knows that youth is vain. *Exit*

TIBERIO.

Why, now I have it, Fawn, the way, the means, and 655
meaning. Good duke, and 'twere not for pity, I could
laugh at thee. Dulcimel, I am thine most miraculously. I
will now begin to sigh, read poets, look pale, go neatly,
and be most apparently in love. As for—

HERCULES.

As for your old father—   660

TIBERIO.

Alas, he and all know, this an old saw hath been,
Faith's breach for love and kingdoms is no sin.   *Exit.*

HERCULES.

Where are we now? Cyllenian Mercury,
And thou quick issue of Jove's broken pate,
Aid and direct us. You better stars to knowledge,   665
Sweet constellations, that affect pure oil
And holy vigil of the pale-cheek'd muses,
Give your best influence, that with able spright
We may correct and please, giving full light
To every angle of this various sense: 670
Works of strong birth end better than commence.   *Exit.*

660. your] *Bullen;* you *Q1–2.*   666. affect] *Q2;* effect *Q1.*
664. issue] *Q2;* messenger *Q1.*   671.1. *Finis Actus quarti Q1–2.*

---

663. *Cyllenian Mercury*] Born on the Arcadian mountain of Cyllene,
Mercury escorts and counsels heroes in dangerous times.
    664. *quick issue . . . pate*] i.e., Athene, who sprang full grown from the
head of Zeus, her father, which Hephaestus (or Prometheus) had opened
with an axe.

[V.i]

Whilst the act is a-playing, Hercules *and* Tiberio *enter;* Tiberio *climbs the tree, and is received above by* Dulcimel, Philocalia, *and a Priest:* Hercules *stays beneath.*

HERCULES.

    Thou mother of chaste dew, night's modest lamp,
    Thou by whose faint shine the blushing lovers
    Join glowing cheeks, and mix their trembling lips
    In vows well kiss'd, rise all as full of splendor
    As my breast is of joy! You genital,   5
    You fruitful well-mix'd heats, O, bless the sheets
    Of yonder chamber, that Ferrara's dukedom,
    The race of princely issue, be not curs'd,
    And ended in abhorred barrenness.
    At length kill all my fears, nor let it rest   10
    Once more my tremblings that my too cold son
    (That ever-scorner of humaner loves)
    Will still contemn the sweets of marriage,
    Still kill our hope of name in his dull coldness.
    Let it be lawful to make use, ye powers,   15
    Of human weakness, that pursueth still
    What is inhibited, and most affects
    What is most difficult to be obtain'd:
    So we may learn, that nicer love's a shade;
    It follows fled, pursu'd flies as afraid;   20
    And in the end close all the various errors
    Of passages most truly comical
    In moral learning, with like confidence
    Of him that vow'd good fortune of the scene
    Shall neither make him fat, or bad make lean.   25

Enter Dondolo *laughing.*

DONDOLO.

    Ha, ha, ha!

HERCULES.

    Why dost laugh, fool? Here's nobody with thee.

12. humaner] *Q2;* humaine *Q1.*   15. powers] *Q2;* sowers *Q1.*
14. kill] *Q2, 1633;* till *Q1.*

DONDOLO.

Why, therefore do I laugh, because there's nobody with me. Would I were a fool alone. I'faith, I am come to attend—let me go, I am sent to the princess—to come and attend her father to the end of Cupid's parliament. 30

HERCULES.

Why, ha' they sat already upon any statutes?

DONDOLO.

Sat? Ay, all's agreed in the nether house.

HERCULES.

Why, are they divided?

DONDOLO.

O ay, in Cupid's parliament all the young gallants are o' 35 the nether house, and all the old signiors that can but only kiss are of the upper house. Is the princess above?

HERCULES.

No, sure, I think the princess is beneath, man. Ha' they supp'd, fool?

DONDOLO.

O yes, the confusion of tongues at the large table is broke 40 up, for see the presence fills. A fool, a fool, a fool, my coxcomb for a fool!

Enter Sir Amoroso, Herod, Nymphadoro, Garbetza, Donetta, *and* Poveia.

HEROD.

Stop, ass. What's matter, idiot?

DONDOLO.

O gallants, my fools that were appointed to wait on Don Cupid have launch'd out their ship to purge their stomachs 45 on the water, and before Jupiter, I fear they will prove defective in their attendance.

HEROD.

Pish, fool, they'll float in with the next tide.

35. o'] *Bullen;* a *Q1–2; in 1633.* 2.
42.1. Amoroso] *Amaros Q1–2.*   42.1. Donetta] *Donella Q1–2.*
42.1. Nymphadoro] *Nymphadon Q1–*

33. *nether*] lower.
41. *presence*] presence chamber.
41–42. *A fool . . .fool!*] a parody of *Richard III,* I.i.32.

DONDOLO.

    Ay, but when's that? Let's see mine almanac or prog-
nostication.   50

SIR AMOROSO.

    What, is this for this year?

DONDOLO.

    In true wisdom, sir, it is. Let me see the moon. 'Fore pity,
'tis in the wane. What grief is this, that so great a planet
should ever decline or lose splendor? Full sea at—

SIR AMOROSO.

    Where's the sign now, fool?   55

DONDOLO.

    In Capricorn, Sir Amoroso.

GARBETZA.

    What strange thing does this almanac speak of, fool?

DONDOLO.

    Is this your lady, Sir Amorous?

SIR AMOROSO.

    It is. Kiss her, fool.

HEROD.

    You may kiss her now. She is married.   60

SIR AMOROSO.

    So he might ha' done before.

DONDOLO.

    In sober modesty, sir, I do not use to do it behind.

HEROD.

    Good fool, be acquainted with this lady too. She's of a very
honest nature, I assure thee.

DONDOLO.

    I easily believe you, sir, for she hath a very vile face, I assure   65
you.

GARBETZA.

    But what strange things does thy almanac speak of, good
fool?

DONDOLO.

    That this year no child shall be begotten but shall have
a true father.   70

65. vile] *Q2;* good *Q1, 1633.*

49–50. *prognostication*] another name for almanac.
55. *sign*] of the zodiac.

SIR AMOROSO.

That's good news, i'faith. I am glad I got my wife with child this year.

HERCULES.

Why, Sir Amorous, this may be, and yet you not the true father. May it not, Herod?

GARBETZA.

But what more says it, good Fawn? 75

HERCULES.

Faith, lady, very strange things. It says that some ladies of your hair shall have feeble hams, short memories, and very weak eyesight, so that they shall mistake their own page, or even brother-in-law, sometimes for their husbands.

SIR AMOROSO.

Is that all, Fawn? 80

HERCULES.

No, Sir Amorous, here's likewise prophesied a great scarcity of gentry to ensue, and that some bores shall be dubbed Sir Amoroso. A great scarcity of lawyers is likewise this year to ensue, so that some one of them shall be entreated to take fees o' both sides. 85

Enter Don Zuccone, *following* Donna Zoya *on his knees.*

ZUCCONE.

Most dear, dear lady! Wife, lady, wife! O do not but look on me, and ha' some mercy!

ZOYA.

I will ha' no mercy. I will not relent.

ZUCCONE.

Sweet lady!

ZOYA.

The order shall stand. I am separated, and I will be 90 separated.

ZUCCONE.

Dear! My love! Wife!

ZOYA.

Hence, fellow! I am none of thy wife. No, I will be tyrannous and a most deep revenger. The order shall stand. I will marry a fellow that keeps a fox in his bosom, a goat under 95

his armholes, and a polecat in his mouth, rather than
re-accept thee.

ZUCCONE.

Alas, by the Lord, lady, what should I say? As Heaven
shall bless me—what should I say?

HEROD.

Kneel and cry, man!   100

ZOYA.

Was I not handsome, generous, honest enough from my
foot to my feather, for such a fellow as thou art?

ZUCCONE.

Alas, I confess, I confess.

ZOYA.

But go thy ways, and wive with whom thou wilt, for my
part. Thou hast spun a fair thread. Who'll kiss thee now? 105
Who'll court thee now? Who'll ha' thee now?

ZUCCONE.

Yet be a woman, and for God's sake help me.

HEROD.

And do not stand too stiffly.

ZUCCONE.

And do not stand too stiffly! Do you make an ass of me?
But let these rascals laugh at me. Alas, what could I do 110
withal? 'Twas my destiny that I should abuse you.

ZOYA.

So it is your destiny that I should thus revenge your abuse.
No, the Irishman shall hate *aqua vitae*, the Welshman
cheese, and the Dutchman salt butter, before I'll love or re-
ceive thee. Does he cry? Does the babe pule? 'Tis too late 115
now. Thou shouldst ha' cried before. 'Tis too late now.
Go bury thy head in silence, and let oblivion be thy utmost
hope.

The Courtiers address themselves to dancing, whilst the Duke *enters with*
Granuffo, *and takes his state.*

HERCULES.

Gallants, to dancing. Loud music, the duke's upon entrance!

113. hate] *Q2, 1633;* eate *Q1.*

118.2. *state*] chair of state, throne.

GONZAGO.

Are the sports ready?   120

HERCULES.

Ready.

GONZAGO.

'Tis enough. Of whose invention is this parliament?

HERCULES.

Ours.

GONZAGO.

'Tis enough.
This night we will exult! O let this night   125
Be ever memoriz'd with prouder triumphs.
Let it be writ in lasting character
That this night our great wisdom did discover
So close a practice—that this night, I say,
Our policy found out, nay, dash'd the drifts   130
Of the young prince, and put him to his shifts,
Nay, past his shifts ('fore Jove! we could make a good
    poet)—
Delight us. On! we deign our princely ear—
We are well pleas'd to grace you; then scorn fear.

Cornets playing. Drunkenness, Sloth, Pride, *and* Plenty *lead* Cupid
to his state, who is followed by Folly, War, Beggary, *and* Laughter.

Stand, 'tis wisdom to acknowledge ignorance   135
Of what we know not. We would not now prove foolish.
Expound the meaning of your show.

HERCULES.

Triumphant Cupid, that sleeps on the soft cheek
Of rarest beauty, whose throne's in ladies' eyes,
Whose force writh'd lightning from Jove's shaking hand,   140
Forc'd strong Alcides to resign his club,
Pluck'd Neptune's trident from his mighty arm,

---

133. deign] *Q2;* dare *Q1.*   *Q1. At l. 145, both Q1–2 print*
134. you] *Q2;* him *Q1.*   Laughter.
134.2. Laughter] *Q2;* Slaughter

---

126. *memoriz'd*] held in memory.
129. *close . . . practice*] secret plot.
141. *Alcides*] Hercules.

Unhelmed Mars: he (with those trophies borne,
Led in by Sloth, Pride, Plenty, Drunkenness,
Follow'd by Folly, War, Laughter, Beggary)   145
Takes his fair throne. Sit pleas'd, for now we move
And speak not for our glory, but for love.

Hercules *takes a bowl of wine.*

GONZAGO.
  A pretty figure.
  What, begins this session with ceremony?
HERCULES.
  With a full health to our great mistress, Venus,   150
  Let every state of Cupid's parliament
  Begin the session, *et quod bonum faustumque sit precor.*

Hercules *drinks a health.*

GONZAGO.
  Give't us, we'll pledge. Nor shall a man that lives,
  In charity refuse it. I will not be so old
  As not be grac'd to honor Cupid. Give't us full.   155
  When we were young we could ha' troll'd it off,
  Drunk down a Dutchman.
HERCULES.
  'Tis lamentable; pity your grace has forgot it. Drunkenness!
  O 'tis a most fluent and swelling virtue, sure the most just
  of all virtues. 'Tis justice itself, for if it chance to oppress 160
  and take too much, it presently restores it again. It makes
  the king and the peasant equal, for if they are both drunk
  alike, they are both beasts alike. As for that most precious
  light of heaven, Truth, if Time be the father of her, I am
  sure Drunkenness is oftentimes the mother of her, and   165
  brings her forth. Drunkenness brings all out, for it brings all
  the drink out of the pot, all the wit out of the pate, and all
  the money out of the purse.

---

143. those] *Q2;* these *Q1.*   152. *et*] *Q1; not in Q2.*

---

152. *et ... precor*] and I pray for what is good and favorable.
156. *troll'd*] "to cause to pass from one to another, especially in phrase
'to troll the bowl'" (*OED*).

GONZAGO.

My Lord Granuffo, this Fawn is an excellent fellow.

DONDOLO.

Silence.   170

GONZAGO.

I warrant you for my lord here.

CUPID.

Since multitude of laws are signs either of much tyranny
in the prince or much rebellious disobedience in the
subject, we rather think it fit to study how to have our old
laws thoroughly executed, than to have new statutes cum- 175
brously invented.

GONZAGO.

Afore Jove, he speaks very well.

HERCULES.

O, sir, Love is very eloquent, makes all men good orators;
himself then must needs be eloquent.

CUPID.

Let it therefore be the main of our assembly to survey our 180
old laws, and punish their transgressions, for that continually
the complaints of lovers ascend up to our deity, that love is
abus'd, and basely bought and sold, beauty corrupted,
affection feign'd, and pleasure herself sophisticated; that
young gallants are proud in appetite and weak in per- 185
formance; that young ladies are phantastically inconstant,
old ladies impudently unsatiate. Wives complain of un-
married women, that they steal the dues belonging to their
sheets; and maids exclaim upon wives, that they unjustly
engross all into their own hands, as not content with their 190
own husbands, but also purloining that which should be
their comfort. Let us therefore be severe in our justice; and
if any of what degree soever have approvedly offended, let
him be instantly unpartially arrested and punished. Read
our statutes.   195

HERCULES.

"A statute made in the five thousand four hundred three-

189. maids] *Q2;* maides make *Q1.*

---

181. *for that*] because.
184. *sophisticated*] adulterated.

score and three year of the easeful reign of the mighty
potent Don Cupid, emperor of sighs and protestations,
great king of kisses, archduke of dalliance, and sole Lord of
Hymen for the maintaining and relieving of his old 200
soldiers, maimed or dismember'd in love."

DONDOLO.

Those that are lightly hurt, shame to complain; those that
are deeply struck are past recovery.

CUPID.

On to the next.

HERCULES.

"An act against the plurality of mistresses."   205

CUPID.

Read.

HERCULES.

"Whereas some over-amorous and unconscionable covetous
young gallants, without all grace of Venus, or the fear of
Cupid in their minds, have at one time engrossed the care or
cures of divers mistresses, with the charge of ladies, into 210
their own tenure or occupation, whereby their mistresses
must of necessity be very ill and unsufficiently served, and
likewise many able portly gallants live unfurnished of
competent entertainment, to the merit of their bodies;
and whereas likewise some other greedy strangers have taken 215
in the purlieus, outset land, and the ancient commons of
our sovereign liege Don Cupid, taking in his very highways,
and enclosing them, and annexing them to their own lord-
ships, to the much impoverishing and putting of divers of
Cupid's true hearts and loyal subjects to base and abomin- 220
able shifts: Be it therefore enacted by the sovereign
authority and erected ensign of Don Cupid, with the assent
of some of the lords, most of the ladies, and all the commons,
that what person or persons soever shall, in the trade of
honor, presume to wear at one time two ladies' favors, or at 225
one time shall earnestly court two women in the way of
marriage, or if any under the degree of a duke shall keep

199–200. Lord of Hymen] *Deighton;*   216. outset] *Q1 corr., Q2, 1633;* a
lou'de of him *Q2;* lou'de of Her *Q1.*   sette *Q1 uncorr.*

216 *purlieus, outset land*] outlying district, formerly forest or commons.

above twenty women of pleasure, a duke's brother fifteen,
a lord ten, a knight or a pensioner or both four, a gentleman
two, shall *ipso facto* be arrested by folly's mace, and instantly   230
committed to the ship of fools, without either bail or mainprize, *Millesimo centesimo quingentesimo quadragesimo nono.*
Cupidinis semper unius." —Nymphadoro, to the bar!

NYMPHADORO.

Shame o' folly, will Fawn now turn an informer? Does he
laugh at me?   235

HERCULES.

Domina Garbetza, did he not ever protest you were his most
only elected mistress?

GARBETZA.

He did.

HERCULES.

Domina Donetta, did he not ever protest you were his most
only elected mistress?   240

DONETTA.

He did.

HERCULES.

Domina Poveia, did he not ever protest, that you were his
most only elected mistress?

POVEIA.

He did.

NYMPHADORO.

Mercy!   245

CUPID.

Our mercy is nothing, unless some lady will beg thee.

LADIES.

Out upon him, dissembling, perfidious liar!

HERCULES.

Indeed 'tis no reason ladies should beg liars.

NYMPHADORO.

Thus he that loveth many, if once known,

239. Donetta] *Donella Q 1–2.*

232–233. *Millesimo ... unius*] parody of legal jargon, part Latin, part
Italian: "A thousand hundred fifty forty eleven times. Always of one
desire."

Is justly plagued to be belov'd of none.   *Exit.* 250
HERCULES.

"An act against counterfeiting of Cupid's royal coin, and
abusing his subjects with false money." —To the bar, Sir
Amorous! —"In most lamentable form complaineth to your
blind celsitude your distressed orators, the women of the
world, that in respect that many spendthrifts, who having 255
exhausted and wasted their substance, and in stranger
parts have with empty shows treasonably purchased ladies'
affections, without being of ability to pay them for it with
current money, and therefore have deceitfully sought to
satisfy them with counterfeit metal, to the great displeasure 260
and no small loss of your humblest subjects: May it therefore with your pitiful assent be enacted, that what lord,
knight, or gentleman soever, knowing himself insufficient,
bankrout, exhausted, and wasted, shall traitorously dare to
entertain any lady as wife or mistress, *ipso facto* to be 265
severed from all commercement with women, his wife or
mistress in that state offending to be forgiven with a
pardon of course, and himself instantly to be pressed to
sail in the ship of fools, without either bail or mainprize."
Sir Amorous is arrested.   270

SIR AMOROSO.

Judgment of the court.

HERCULES.

I take my oath upon thy brother's body, 'tis none of thine.

SIR AMOROSO.

By the heart of dissemblance, this Fawn has wrought with
us as strange tailors work in corporate cities, where they
are not free. All inward, inward he lurk'd in the bosom of 275
us, and yet we know not his profession. Sir, let me have
counsel!

HERCULES.

'Tis in great Cupid's case; you may have no counsel.

250. belov'd] *Q2, 1633;* beleeu'de   Sir iudgement *Q1.*
Q1.   271. court] *Q2;* countrie *Q1.*
269. prize."] prise. *Herc. Q1–2.*   278. great Cupid's] *Q2;* great *Q1;*
271. SIR AMOROSO. Judgment] Sir   a great *1633.*
Amar Iudgement *Q2; Don, Amar.*

254. *celsitude*] loftiness.   264. *bankrout*] bankrupt.

SIR AMOROSO.

Death o' justice! Are we in Normandy? What is my lady's
doom then?   280

CUPID.

Acquitted by the express parole of the statute. Hence, and
in thy ignorance be quietly happy. Away with him. On!

HERCULES.

"An act against forgers of love letters, false braggarts of
ladies' favors, and vain boasters of counterfeit tokens."

HEROD.

'Tis I, 'tis I, I confess guilty, guilty.   285

HERCULES.

I will be most humane and right courteously languaged in
thy correction, and only say, thy vice, from apparent heir,
has made thee an apparent beggar, and now of a false
knave hath made thee a true fool. Folly, to the ship with him
and twice a day let him be duck'd at the main yard.   290

CUPID.

Proceed.

HERCULES.

"An act against slanderers of Cupid's liege, ladies' names,
and lewd defamers of their honors."

ZUCCONE.

'Tis I, 'tis I, I weep and cry out, I have been a most
contumelious offender. My only cry is *miserere*.   295

CUPID.

If your relenting lady will have pity on you, the fault
against our deity be pardoned.

ZUCCONE.

Madam, if ever I have found favor in your eyes, if ever
you have thought me a reasonable handsome fellow, as I
am sure before I had a beard you might, O be merciful!   300

ZOYA.

Well, upon your apparent repentance, that all modest

279. SIR AMOROSO. Death] *Sir Amor.*   penaltie *Q1.*
death *Q2; Don. Amor.* Sir death *Q1.*   287. from] *Q2; not in Q1.*
281. express parole] *Q2;* right   287. heir] *this edn.;* here *Q1-2.*

295. *miserere*] have˝mercy.

spectators may witness I have for a short time only
thus feignedly hated you that you might ever after truly
love me, upon these cautions I re-accept you: first you shall
vow—   305

ZUCCONE.

I do vow, as heaven bless me, I will do—

ZOYA.

What?

ZUCCONE.

Whate'er it be. Say on, I beseech you.

ZOYA.

You shall vow—

ZUCCONE.

Yes.   310

ZOYA.

That you shall never—

ZUCCONE.

Never—

ZOYA.

Feign love to my waiting-woman or chambermaid.

ZUCCONE.

No.

ZOYA.

Never promise them such a farm to their marriage—   315

ZUCCONE.

No.

ZOYA.

If she'll discover but whom I affect.

ZUCCONE.

Never.

ZOYA.

Or if they know none, that they'll but take a false oath I do,
only to be rid of me.   320

ZUCCONE.

I swear I will not. I will not only not counterfeitly love
your women, but I will truly hate them; an't be possible,
so far from maintaining them, that I will beggar them.

---

315. *farm*] income.

I will never pick their trunks for letters, search their
pockets, ruffle their bosoms, or tear their foul smocks; never, 325
never!

ZOYA.

That if I chance to have a humor to be in a masque, you
shall not grow jealous.

ZUCCONE.

Never.

ZOYA.

Or grudge at the expense.   330

ZUCCONE.

Never! I will eat mine own arms first.

ZOYA.

That you shall not search, if my chamber-door hinges be
oil'd to avoid creaking.

ZUCCONE.

As I am a sensible creature—

ZOYA.

Nor ever suspect the reason why my bedchamber floor is 335
doubled-matted.

ZUCCONE.

Not as I have blood in me.

ZOYA.

You shall vow to wear clean linen, and feed wholesomely.

ZUCCONE.

Ay, and highly. I will take no more tobacco, or come to
your sheets drunk, or get wenches. I will ever feed on fried 340
frogs, broil'd snails, and boil'd lambstones. I will adore
thee more than a mortal, observe and serve you as more
than a mistress, do all duties of a husband, all offices of a
man, all services of thy creature, and ever live in thy
pleasure, or die in thy service.   345

ZOYA.

Then here my quarrel ends. Thus cease all strife.

ZUCCONE.

Until they lose, men know not what's a wife.

341. broil'd] *Q2;* wild *Q1.*

---

343. *offices*] duties.
344. *creature*] servant (cf. III.i.300.n.).

We slight and dully view the lamp of heaven,
Because we daily see't, which but bereaved,
And held one little week from darkened eyes,   350
With greedy wonder we should all admire.
Opinion of command puts out love's fire.

HERCULES.

"An act against mummers, false seemers, that abuse ladies
with counterfeit faces, courting only by signs, and seeming
wise only by silence."   355

CUPID.

The penalty?

HERCULES.

To be urged to speak, and then, if inward ability answer
not outward seeming, to be committed instantly to the
ship of fools during great Cupid's pleasure. —My Lord
Granuffo, to the bar! Speak, speak, is not this law just?   360

GRANUFFO.

Just, sure; for in good truth or in good sooth,
When wise men speak, they still must open their mouth.

HERCULES.

The brazen head has spoken.

DONDOLO.

Thou art arrested.

GRANUFFO.

Me?   365

HERCULES.

And judg'd. Away!   *Exit* Granuffo.

GONZAGO.

Thus silence and grave looks, with hums and haws,
Makes many worship'd, when if tried th'are daws.
That's the morality or *l'envoy* of it—
L'envoy of it. On.   370

HERCULES.

"An act against privy conspiracies, by which if any with
ambitious wisdom shall hope and strive to outstrip Love,

---

352. Opinion] *Q2;* And prowde   367. and grave] *Q2;* can enuie *Q1.*
hayht *Q1;* And proud height *1633.*   368. th'are] *Q2;* were *Q1.*

---

349. *bereaved*] deprived.
363. *brazen . . . spoken*] see I.ii.118.n.

to cross his words, and make frustrate his sweet pleasures,
if such a presumptuous wisdom fall to nothing, and die in
laughter, the wizard so transgressing is *ipso facto* adjudged 375
to offend in most deep treason, to forfeit all his wit at the
will of the lord, and be instantly committed to the ship of
fools for ever."

GONZAGO.

Ay, marry, sir! O might Oedipus riddle me out such a
fellow! Of all creatures breathing, I do hate those things 380
that struggle to seem wise, and yet are indeed very fools.
I remember when I was a young man in my father's days,
there were four gallant spirits for resolution, as proper
for body, as witty in discourse as any were in Europe,
nay Europe had not such. I was one of them. We four did 385
all love one lady, a modest, chaste virgin she was. We all
enjoy'd her, I well remember, and so enjoy'd her that,
despite the strictest guard was set upon her, we had her
at our pleasure. I speak it for her honor and my credit.
Where shall you find such witty fellows nowadays? Alas, 390
how easy it is in these weaker times to cross love-tricks. Ha,
ha, ha! Alas, alas, I smile to think I must confess with some
glory to mine own wisdom, to think how I found out, and
crossed and curb'd, and jerk'd and firk'd, and in the end
made desperate Tiberio's hope. Alas, good silly youth, 395
that dares to cope with age and such a beard. I speak it
without glory.

HERCULES.

But what yet might your well-known wisdom think,
If such a one, as being most severe,
A most protested opposite to the match   400
Of two young lovers—who having barr'd them speech,
All interviews, all messages, all means,
To plot their wished ends—even he himself
Was by their cunning made the go-between,
The only messenger, the token-carrier,   405
Told them the times when they might fitly meet,
Nay, show'd the way to one another's bed?

---

379. *Oedipus*] who was able to answer the riddle of the Sphynx.
394. *firk'd*] trounced.

GONZAGO.

May one have the sight of such a fellow for nothing?
Doth there breathe such an egregious ass?
Is there such a foolish animal in *rerum natura*?   410
How is it possible such a simplicity can exist? Let us not
lose our laughing at him, for God's sake! Let Folly's scepter
light upon him, and to the ship of fools with him instantly.

DONDOLO.

Of all these follies I arrest your grace.

GONZAGO.

Me? Ha! Me? Me, varlet? Me, fool? Ha! to th' jail with 415
him! What, varlet? Call me ass? —Me?

HERCULES.

What, grave Urbin's duke?
Dares Folly's scepter touch his prudent shoulders?
Is he a coxcomb? No, my lord is wise,
For we all know that Urbin's duke has eyes.   420

GONZAGO.

God a-mercy, Fawn! Hold, varlet!
Hold thee, good Fawn! —Railing reprobate!

HERCULES.

Indeed, I must confess your grace did tell
And first did intimate your daughter's love
To otherwise most cold Tiberio;   425
After convey'd her private favor to him,
A curious scarf, wherein her needle wrought
Her private love to him.

GONZAGO   What! I do this? Ha!

HERCULES.

And last, by her persuasion, show'd the youth
The very way and best-elected time   430
To come unto her chamber.

GONZAGO.   Thus did I, sir?

HERCULES.

Thus did you, sir. But I must confess
You meant not to do this, but were rankly gull'd,

409. breathe] *Bullen;* breath *Q1-2.*   428. love] *Q2;* fauour *Q1.*
421. Hold] *Q2;* hold fast *Q1.*

410. *rerum natura*] the nature of things.

Made a plain natural. This sure, sir, you did.
And in assurance, Prince Tiberio,   435
Renowned, witted Dulcimel, appear!
The acts of constant honor cannot fear.   Hercules *Exit*.

Tiberio *and* Dulcimel *above are discoverd hand in hand.*

DULCIMEL.

Royally wise, and wisely royal father—

DONDOLO.

That's sententious now, a figure call'd in art *Ironia*.

DULCIMEL.

I humbly thank your worthy piety   440
That through your only means I have obtained
So fit, loving, and desired a husband.

GONZAGO.

Death o' discretion! if I should prove a fool now. Am not
I an ass, think you, ha? I will have them both bound
together, and sent to the Duke of Ferrara presently.   445

TIBERIO.

I am sure, good father, we are both bound together as fast
as the priest can make us already. I thank you for it, kind
father. I thank you only for't.

Hercules *enters in his own shape.*

HERCULES.

And as for sending them to the Duke of Ferrara, see, my
good lord, Ferrara's o'erjoy'd prince meets them in fullest 450
wish.

GONZAGO.

By the Lord, I am asham'd of myself, that's the plain troth.
But I know now wherefore this parliament was. What a

439. a figure call'd in] *Q2; not in*   453. parliament] *Q2; not in Q1.*
Q1.

---

434. *natural*] a simpleton.
439. *Ironia*] "Ye doe likewise dissemble, when ye speake in derision or
mockerie, & that may be many waies: as sometime in sport, sometime in
earnest, and privily, and apertly, and pleasantly, and bitterly: but first
by the figure *Ironia*, which we call the *drye mock* . . .." (George Puttenham,
The Arte of English Poesie, edited by Gladys Doidge Willcock and Alice
Walker, Cambridge, 1936, p. 189.)

slumber have I been in!

HERCULES.

Never grieve or wonder. All things sweetly fit.   455

GONZAGO.

There is no folly to protested wit.

HERCULES.

What still in wond'ring ignorance doth rest,
In private conference your dear-lov'd breast
Shall fully take. —But now we change our face.

EPILOGUS

And thus in bold yet modest phrase we end.
He whose Thalia with swiftest hand hath penn'd
This lighter subject, and hath boldly torn
Fresh bays from Daphne's arm, doth only scorn
Malicious censures of some envious few,   5
Who think they lose if others have their due.
But let such adders hiss; know, all the sting,
All the vain foam of all those snakes that rings
Minerva's glassful shield, can never taint,
Poison, or pierce; firm art disdains to faint.   10
But yet of you that with impartial faces,
With no prepared malice, but with graces
Of sober knowledge, have survey'd the frame
Of his slight scene, if you shall judge his flame
Distemperately weak, as faulty much   15
In style, in plot, in spirit; lo! if such,
He deigns, in self-accusing phrase, to crave
Not praise, but pardon, which he hopes to have;
    Since he protests he ever hath aspir'd
    To be belov'd, rather than admir'd.   20

FINIS

455. fit] *Q2;* still *Q1.*   [Epilogus]
456. wit] *Q2;* will *Q1.*   18. Not] *Bullen;* For *Q1–2.*

---

456. *to*] compared to.
[Epilogus]
  2. *Thalia*] muse of comedy.

Appendix

Chronology

Approximate years are indicated by*, occurrences in doubt by (?).

Political and Literary Events	Life and Major Works of Marston
1558	
Accession of Queen Elizabeth.	
Robert Greene born.	
Thomas Kyd born.	
1560	
George Chapman born.	
1561	
Francis Bacon born.	
1564	
Shakespeare born.	
Christopher Marlowe born.	
1570	
Thomas Heywood born.*	
1572	
Thomas Dekker born.*	
John Donne born.	
Massacre of St. Bartholomew's Day.	
1573	
Ben Jonson born.*	
1576	
The Theatre, the first permanent public theater in London, established by James Burbage.	John Marston born, only son of lawyer John Marston and Marie Guarsi, of Italian extraction.
1577	
The Curtain theater opened.	
Holinshed's *Chronicles of England, Scotland and Ireland*.	
Drake begins circumnavigation of the earth; completed 1580.	

1578
John Lyly's *Euphues: The Anatomy of Wit.*

1579
John Fletcher born.
Sir Thomas North's translation of Plutarch's *Lives*

1580
Thomas Middleton born.

1583
Philip Massinger born.

1584
Francis Beaumont born.*

1586
Death of Sir Philip Sidney.
John Ford born.

1587
The Rose theater opened by Henslowe.
Marlowe's *TAMBURLAINE*, Part I.*
Execution of Mary, Queen of Scots.
Drake raids Cadiz.

1588
Defeat of the Spanish Armada.
Marlowe's *TAMBURLAINE*, Part II.*

1589
Greene's *FRIAR BACON AND FRIAR BUNGAY.*
Marlowe's *THE JEW OF MALTA.*
Kyd's *THE SPANISH TRAGEDY.*

1590
Spenser's *Faerie Queene* (Books I–III) published.
Sidney's *Arcadia* published.
Shakespeare's *HENRY VI*, Parts I–III,* *TITUS ANDRONICUS.*

1591
Shakespeare's *RICHARD III.*   Enters Brasenose College, Oxford (?).

1592

Marlowe's *DOCTOR FAUSTUS** and *EDWARD II.**
Shakespeare's *TAMING OF THE SHREW** and *THE COMEDY OF ERRORS.**
Death of Greene.

Matriculates at Brasenose College. Member of the Middle Temple, London.

1593

Shakespeare's *LOVE'S LABOUR'S LOST;** *Venus and Adonis* published.
Death of Marlowe.
Theaters closed on account of plague.

1594

Shakespeare's *TWO GENTLE-MEN OF VERONA;** *The Rape of Lucrece* published.
Shakespeare's company becomes Lord Chamberlain's Men.
James Shirley born.*
Death of Kyd.

Graduates B.A.

1595

The Swan theater built.
Sidney's *Defense of Poesy* published.
Shakespeare's *ROMEO AND JULIET,** *A MIDSUMMER NIGHT'S DREAM,** *RICHARD II.**
Raleigh's first expedition to Guiana.

Residing in the Middle Temple.

1596

Spenser's *Faerie Queene* (Books IV–VI) published.
Shakespeare's *MERCHANT OF VENICE,** *KING JOHN.**

1597

Bacon's *Essays* (first edition).
Shakespeare's *HENRY IV*, Part I.*

1598

Demolition of The Theatre.
Shakespeare's *MUCH ADO ABOUT NOTHING,** *HENRY IV*, Part II.*
Jonson's *EVERY MAN IN HIS HUMOR* (first version).

The Metamorphosis of Pygmalion's Image and *The Scourge of Villainy.*

Seven books of Chapman's translation of Homer's *Iliad* published.

1599

The Paul's Boys reopen their theater.
The Globe theater opened.
Shakespeare's *AS YOU LIKE IT*,* *HENRY V, JULIUS CAESAR.**
Dekker's *THE SHOEMAKERS' HOLIDAY.**
Death of Spenser.

HISTRIOMASTIX,* *ANTONIO AND MELLIDA*,* Parts I and II.

1600

Shakespeare's *TWELFTH NIGHT.**
The Fortune theater built by Alleyn.
The Children of the Chapel begin to play at the Blackfriars.

*JACK DRUM'S ENTERTAIN-MENT.**

1601

Shakespeare's *HAMLET*,* *MERRY WIVES OF WINDSOR.**
Insurrection and execution of the Earl of Essex.
Jonson's *POETASTER* (ridiculing Marston).

WHAT YOU WILL,* *SATIRO-MASTIX* (? with Dekker).*

1602

Shakespeare's *TROILUS AND CRESSIDA.**

1603

Death of Queen Elizabeth; accession of James VI of Scotland as James I.
Florio's translation of Montaigne's *Essays* published.
Shakespeare's *ALL'S WELL THAT ENDS WELL.**
Heywood's *A WOMAN KILLED WITH KINDNESS.*
Shakespeare's company becomes the King's Men.

THE MALCONTENT * (played by the Queen's Revels company of boys, at the Blackfriars—a company in which Marston had acquired shares; stolen and acted by the King's Men at the Globe).

1604

Shakespeare's *MEASURE FOR MEASURE*,* *OTHELLO.**
Chapman's *BUSSY D'AMBOIS.**

THE FAWN,* *THE DUTCH COURTESAN.**

1605

Shakespeare's *KING LEAR.**
Bacon's *Advancement of Learning*
published.
The Gunpowder Plot.

EASTWARD HO* (with Jonson and
Chapman).
Marries Mary Wilkes of Barford,
Wilts.

1606

Shakespeare's *MACBETH.**
Jonson's *VOLPONE.**
Tourneur's *REVENGER'S TRAG-
EDY.**
The Red Bull theater built.
Death of John Lyly.

SOPHONISBA.*
The City Pageant.

1607

Shakespeare's *ANTONY AND
CLEOPATRA.**
Beaumont's *KNIGHT OF THE
BURNING PESTLE.**
Settlement of Jamestown, Virginia.

The Ashby Entertainment.
THE INSATIATE COUNTESS*
(completed by William Barksted).

1608

Shakespeare's *CORIOLANUS,**
TIMON OF ATHENS,* *PERI-
CLES.**
Chapman's *CONSPIRACY AND
TRAGEDY OF CHARLES, DUKE
OF BYRON.**
Dekker's *Gull's Hornbook* published.
Richard Burbage leases Blackfriars
Theatre for King's company.
John Milton born.

Committed to Newgate prison by
the Privy Council (for reasons
unknown).

1609

Shakespeare's *CYMBELINE;** *Sonnets* published.
Jonson's *EPICOENE.*

Ordained deacon and then priest.

1610

Jonson's *ALCHEMIST.*
Chapman's *REVENGE OF BUSSY
D'AMBOIS.**
Richard Crashaw born.

1611

Authorized (King James) Version
of the Bible published.
Shakespeare's *THE WINTER'S
TALE,** *THE TEMPEST.**

Beaumont and Fletcher's *A KING
AND NO KING*
Tourneur's *ATHEIST'S TRAG-
EDY.**
Middleton's *A CHASTE MAID IN
CHEAPSIDE.*
Chapman's translation of *Iliad*
completed.

1612
Webster's *THE WHITE DEVIL.**

1613
The Globe theater burned.
Shakespeare's *HENRY VIII* (with
Fletcher).
Webster's *THE DUCHESS OF
MALFI.**
Sir Thomas Overbury murdered.

1614
The Globe theater rebuilt.
The Hope Theatre built.
Jonson's *BARTHOLOMEW FAIR.*

1616
Publication of Folio edition of   Vicar of Christchurch, Hants.
Jonson's *Works.*
Chapman's *Whole Works of Homer.*
Death of Shakespeare.
Death of Beaumont.

1618
Outbreak of Thirty Years War.
Execution of Raleigh.

1620
Pilgrim Fathers land at Plymouth.

1621
Middleton's *WOMEN BEWARE
WOMEN.**
Robert Burton's *Anatomy of Mel-
ancholy* published.
Andrew Marvell born.

1622
Middleton and Rowley's *THE
CHANGELING.**
Henry Vaughan born.

1623
Publication of Folio edition of Shakespeare's *COMEDIES, HISTORIES, AND TRAGEDIES.*

1625
Death of King James I; accession of Charles I.
Death of Fletcher.

1626
Death of Tourneur.
Death of Bacon.

1627
Death of Middleton.

1628
Ford's *THE LOVER'S MELANCHOLY.*
Petition of Right.
Buckingham assassinated.

1621
Shirley's *THE TRAITOR.*   Resigns his living of Christchurch.
Death of Donne.
John Dryden born.

1632
Massinger's *THE CITY MADAM.**

1633
Donne's *Poems* published.
Death of George Herbert.

1634
Death of Chapman, Webster.*   Death of Marston.
THE TWO NOBLE KINSMEN published (with title page ascription to Shakespeare and Fletcher).
Milton's *Comus.*

1635
Sir Thomas Browne's *Religio Medici.*

1637
Death of Jonson.

1639
First Bishops' War.
Death of Carew.*

1640
Short Parliament.
Long Parliament impeaches Laud.
Death of Massinger, Burton.

1641
Irish rebel.
Death of Heywood.

1642
Charles I leaves London; Civil War
breaks out.
Shirley's *COURT SECRET*.
All theaters closed by Act of
Parliament.

1643
Parliament swears to the Solemn
League and Covenant.

1645
Ordinance for New Model Army
enacted.

1646
End of First Civil War.

1647
Army occupies London.
Charles I forms alliance with Scots.
Publication of Folio edition of
Beaumont and Fletcher's *COM-
EDIES AND TRAGEDIES*.